Authoring Books and Materials for Students, Academics, and Professionals

Authoring Books and Materials for Students, Academics, and Professionals

Franklin H. Silverman

PRAEGER

Westport, Connecticut
London

Library of Congress Cataloging-in-Publication Data

Silverman, Franklin H., 1933–
    Authoring books and materials for students, academics, and
professionals / Franklin H. Silverman.
      p.   cm.
    Includes bibliographical references and index.
    ISBN 0–275–96159–1 (alk. paper).—ISBN 0–275–96160–5 (pbk. :
alk. paper)
    1. Authorship. I. Title.
PN146.S55   1998
808'.02—dc21   97–44875

British Library Cataloguing in Publication Data is available.

Library of Congress Catalog Card Number: 97–44875
ISBN: 0–275–96159–1
      0–275–96160–5 (pbk.)

First published in 1998

Praeger Publishers, 88 Post Road West, Westport, CT 06881
An imprint of Greenwood Publishing Group, Inc.

Printed in the United States of America

The paper used in this book complies with the
Permanent Paper Standard issued by the National
Information Standards Organization (Z39.48–1984).

10 9 8 7 6 5 4 3 2 1

To Mike Keedy, professor emeritus of mathematics at Purdue University and founder of the Text and Academic Authors Association, for his encouragement and support for both my workshop and this book.

Contents

Preface

Many teachers and other professionals, like yourself, have "played with the idea" of authoring a textbook or professional reference book. Before you can make an informed decision about authoring one, you need information about the ways that you can be both helped and hurt by doing so. And if you decide that the benefits are likely to outweigh the losses, you will need certain information about the publishing industry to maximize the probability that your book will yield adequate financial and other rewards. Both types of information are furnished here in a style that is both conversational and candid. Most of it, incidentally, also is applicable to authoring and publishing educational and professional materials, including computer software, audio tapes, videotapes, diagnostic tests, and sets of teaching or therapy materials.

The content of this book mirrors that of a six-hour workshop that I have been offering since the mid-1980s for persons who are contemplating authoring a professional reference book or textbook. This workshop has been presented under the auspices of several universities and the Text and Academic Authors Association. Participants in it have included faculty from colleges and universities, junior colleges, and high schools, as well as working professionals. The disciplines in which they worked or taught included the physical sciences, biological sciences, behavioral sciences, humanities, education, and the health-care professions. Most of them had an idea for a book but did not know how to proceed. Specifically, they were seeking information about such aspects of authorship and publishing as the qualifications publishers expect their authors to possess, what they can gain and lose by authoring a book (e.g., the amount of income a book is likely to generate and the impact that authoring a book can have on tenure decisions), identifying potential publishers, preparing a proposal, negotiating a contract, strategies that can facilitate writing a book-length manuscript and preparing illustrations, the process involved in transforming a manuscript into a book, how textbooks and professional books are marketed, and business implications of authorship (e.g., will the IRS allow them to deduct the cost of maintaining offices in their homes). All of these topics and issues are dealt with in this book.

Much of the information about a particular topic or issue (e.g., negotiating a contract) is in the chapter that deals with it. However, there may also be information pertinent to it in other chapters. There are, for example, comments concerning contract negotiation in Chapter 3. Consequently, the index is a more useful tool than the table of contents for locating information about some topics and issues.

I interviewed a number of experienced textbook and professional book authors about some of the topics and issues that are discussed in this book. Some excerpts from these interviews that either augment or clarify my discussion are included.

It isn't possible to give credit to the many sources from which the ideas in this book have been drawn. This book is the result of years of involvement with writing and publishing and hundreds of hours of conversation with persons engaged in these activities, particularly members of the Text and Academic Authors Association. Thus, I cannot credit this or that idea to a specific person, but I can say "thank you" to all whose ideas I have borrowed.

An Author's Prayer

Oh God, who hast hitherto supported me, enable me to proceed in this labour, and in the whole task of my present state; that when I shall render up, at the last day, an account of the talent committed to me, I may receive pardon, . . . Amen.*

—Samuel Johnson

*Written on April 3, 1753, the day Johnson began working on the second volume of his dictionary.

1

Qualifications Necessary for Authoring a Textbook or Other Academic or Professional Book or Material

Authoring a textbook, professional book, or other academic book or material almost always requires a large time/energy/ego investment. There are a number of questions you need to answer before you can make an informed decision about whether it is sensible for you to try to undertake such a project at this time. Certainly one of the first of these questions should be the following: "How likely is it that I have the qualifications necessary to interest a publisher in my project?" There are qualifications that really are necessary both to interest a publisher in and successfully complete such a project. There also are qualifications that you might regard as being necessary but that really aren't. Both types are dealt with in this chapter.

One of the first qualifications that you might regard as being necessary is having a national or international reputation as an authority on the topic. Suppose that most prospective consumers of your book or material would not regard you as being one. Does this mean that you are unlikely to be offered a contract by a "respectable" publisher? Absolutely not. Although it certainly helps to be well known and respected in the area (or on the topic) about which you are writing, publishing contracts have been awarded to people who had not yet established a national reputation in the area. Indeed, many textbooks, professional books, and scholarly books have been written by people who had little actual knowledge of the topics that were being dealt with before preparing the proposal. In fact, for three of my books (all of which were published by Prentice Hall), I knew little about the topic before preparing the proposal. Many persons who have authored books and are widely regarded as authorities on the topics with which their books dealt developed their reputations after their books were published.

Another concern that you may have is whether you can write well enough. You have to be able to write clearly—to communicate your ideas in ways that can be easily understood by readers. This ability, of course, is also needed to be a good teacher. Furthermore, you have to be able to present information in a manner that will hold the reader's interest—one that he or she is likely to regard as interesting. This too is needed to be a good teacher. Consequently, the communication abilities needed to write a good textbook, professional book, scholarly book, or other educational material and those needed to be a good teacher are the same. Only the medium is different.

There are some writing abilities that you may consider necessary that really aren't. You don't have to be able to write "artistically" (like a short-story writer or novelist). Furthermore, you don't need to have an extremely large vocabulary, or be a superior speller, or be exceptionally knowledgeable about grammatical usage. Almost all (perhaps all) of the mistakes that you make in these areas and do not detect will be corrected by the person who copyedits the manuscript. If your writing abilities are adequate for authoring reports that reflect well on you and your institution, they probably also are adequate for authoring professional and educational books and materials.

Another concern that you may have about taking on a book or educational material project is whether the time you can devote to the project is likely to be adequate to complete it. You may assume that to complete such a project it is necessary to have large blocks of time available frequently for writing. Although it certainly is helpful to have them, they are not essential. You can successfully complete a book or educational material project by writing a little almost every day. The time you spend each day writing can be as little as 30 minutes (see chapter 6).

There are several qualifications that are essential. They pertain to personality attributes. The first is the ability to stick to a task from which you get little immediate gratification. It is likely to take you more than a year to complete a book project, and there will be days when you won't receive much positive reinforcement from working on it. These may be the days when the writing doesn't seem to "flow" or ones when you discover that paragraphs you thought were well written require further revision. If you are a person who will allow almost nothing to stand in your way once you commit yourself to achieving a goal, you have at least one of these attributes.

Another essential trait for success as an author is being able to tolerate being alone. You will be spending a great deal of time by yourself even if you have co-authors. Writing, ordinarily, is not an activity you can share with others. If you do not enjoy spending time alone, you may have difficulty motivating yourself to stick to a writing schedule.

A third attribute that is essential for success as an educational book or material author is not being overly perfectionistic. If you feel compelled to make a sentence perfect (with respect to grammar, word choice, spelling, and the like) before writing the next one, you probably won't write very much. Most experienced book authors first get their chapters down in rough form and then refine (edit) them.

Although these personality attributes can significantly influence how likely you are to complete an educational book or material project, what is perhaps a more important determiner is your level of *motivation* for doing so, for example, the priority you assign to the project. The following comments by four experienced authors whom I interviewed at a Text and Academic Authors Association (TAA) convention speak to this point:

> If you're going to author books it has to be something you really want to do—something you are doing for love of what you're doing.

> You have to establish your priorities. If writing a textbook is an important thing in your life, you have to give it a place of priority. And you have to establish hours when you must be left alone. Your children must understand they must not interfere with daddy while he is in the bedroom with the door closed. Some professors I've known built little structures in the backyard in order to have a place to write where they wouldn't be interrupted.

> You must be so dedicated that you are willing to spend one to three years developing the project. You must strongly believe that you have something terribly important to tell the world about. It isn't the money. It isn't anything except a strong belief that it must be told and you're the person who can do it.

Authoring a book is a tremendously time-consuming job. You're going to be working evenings, weekends, and Christmas holidays. You're going to be getting up early in the morning and staying up late at night. It's just a very time-consuming business. Every time I have said that to a co-author, in retrospect they said "Oh, I thought I understood what you said, but I didn't." So I don't think that there are any words adequate to tell a prospective author how time consuming it is. They seem to be so eager to do it that they don't hear you.

As these comments indicate, you must be willing to make a significant time and comfort investment. The time investment can be several years. Furthermore, you will have to work on the book when the writing is not going well or when the task you are doing is not enjoyable. There are tasks associated with book writing, such as indexing and proofreading, that few authors enjoy.

People usually don't invest unless they anticipate receiving a meaningful payoff for doing so. It doesn't seem to matter whether the payoff they anticipate is realistic. People who regularly buy state lottery tickets expect to win someday even though the odds against their winning are astronomical.

Your motivation to complete an educational book or material project is unlikely to be adequate if you don't believe strongly that doing so will significantly improve your life. Answer the following hypothetical questions as honestly as you can: "If you were to wake up some morning and find that your book or material had been published, what effect would it have on your life?" "What opportunities would you have that you don't have now?" "How would it affect your self-concept?" "What impacts would it have on your professional and social life?" "Could it in any way affect you adversely?" If your answers to these questions indicate that your completing the project would probably make your life better in some very significant (for you) way or ways, your level of motivation to do what is necessary to complete it is likely to be adequate.

2

Potential Benefits and Losses: Financial and Other

Before deciding to undertake a book or educational material project, you should give some serious thought to whether the potential benefits to you, at this time, are likely to outweigh the potential losses. I will provide at least some of the information that you need to "weigh" them in this chapter.

POTENTIAL BENEFITS

There are a number of benefits (rewards) that you could derive from authoring an educational book or material, including the following: earning additional income, contributing to your field, enhancing your professional reputation, reducing the probability of "burnout," pursuing an activity you enjoy, and improving your teaching skills. Each of these is commented on in this section.

Financial Rewards

One of the main benefits that you would probably expect to derive from authoring educational books or materials is extra income. It is one of the two reasons that was mentioned most often in a 1991 survey of

350 college textbook authors conducted by Publishing Directions. (The other was "improved teaching vehicle.") I am assuming here that you would not quit your job and work full time on the project. Judging by the membership of the Text and Academic Authors Association (TAA), the professional/trade association for creators of academic intellectual property in the United States, very few people do so. More than 90 percent of TAA members have a full-time teaching position or had one before they retired.

Several factors will determine the amount of income you will receive from sales of your book or material. The first is the number of *new* copies that are sold. Obviously, the higher this number, the more income you will receive. The word "new" is highlighted because of the impact that the used-book market has on sales, particularly on those of college textbooks. Many of the respondents in the survey of college textbook authors referred to previously indicated that the sale of used books had significantly reduced their royalty income. Some firms buy textbooks from students and faculty (examination copies) and sell them to college bookstores at a price that enables the bookstores to make more profit from selling used books than they can from selling new ones. One reason that these firms can wholesale books so cheaply is that they do not pay authors a royalty. Consequently, a year after a college textbook is published—particularly if it is for a lower-division undergraduate course—more than half the copies sold are likely to be used ones. Sales of new copies after two or three years probably will only be a small fraction of what they were the first year. Publishers cope with this situation by charging relatively high prices and publishing new editions frequently (sometimes as often as every two or three years).

A second factor that influences your income from an educational book or material project is the amount that you receive for each copy sold. If you are not self-publishing, this is determined by both the percentage you receive as a royalty and the percentage you receive from sales of publication rights. The latter includes sales of translation rights, sales to professional book clubs, and permission fees for reproducing text and/or illustrations from your book or material (e.g., a chapter that a professor includes in a coursepack). Your royalties will be based either on net or on list (retail) price. If it is based on the former, it will probably be specified in the contract as a percentage of the income received by the publisher from sales of the book or material. Most textbook publishers now base royalties on money received. As textbooks and professional books are sold to college bookstores at a discount, you would have to receive a higher royalty percentage to make the same amount on each book if your royalty was based on net rather than list price. For example, a 15 percent royalty rate based on list price would be equivalent to an 18.75 one based on net price (Keedy, 1989).

The royalty percentage you receive may be fixed or variable. If it is fixed, you will receive the same royalty percentage for the first copy sold as for the ten-thousandth one. If it is variable, you will receive a lower royalty percentage for the first one than you will for the ten-thousandth one. The fixed percentage you are most likely to be offered for a book ranges from 8 to 18 percent. The larger the market, the higher this percentage is likely to be. It would tend to be higher, for example, for a lower-division undergraduate textbook than for an upper-division one. A survey conducted by the TAA in 1990 indicated that the most frequent fixed percentage received by authors of college textbooks was 15 percent. The most frequent variable royalty rates they received were either the two step (12.5 percent on the first 3,000 copies of each edition and 15 percent from then on) or the three step (10 percent on the first 2,500 copies of each edition, 12.5 percent on the next 2,500 copies, and 15 percent thereafter). More of the contracts reported on specified a fixed royalty percentage than a variable one.

Another possible source of income from your book or material is *rights sales*. Your publisher may sell a foreign publisher the right to translate it and publish an edition of a particular size. Or your publisher may sell a professional book club the right to print and distribute a certain number of copies. Or your publisher may sell another author the right to include illustrations or text (including whole chapters) from it in his or her book. You will receive a percentage of the income your publisher receives from such sales (usually at least 50 percent).

Some publishers, *if asked*, will give an author an *advance* on royalty and rights income. The contract will specify that it is to be repaid (following publication) from money owed the author. The advance is actually an interest-free loan the publisher makes to the author. The size of the advance can significantly influence the income from a book, particularly if it does not sell well. If the total amount of royalty and rights income generated by a book is less than the amount the author received as an advance, he or she ordinarily does not have to repay the unearned portion to the publisher. It is desirable, therefore, to get as large an advance as you can.

The size of the advance also can influence the income from a book or educational material in another way. The author receives the advance at least a year or two before the first royalty check. By investing it, the author can earn additional income.

Another factor that influences the amount a book will earn is its price. This is set by the publisher and the bookstore. The publisher sets the net (wholesale) price, and the bookstore sets the retail price. Consequently, the prices charged for a particular college textbook on different campuses may not be the same. The publisher is given the right in the publishing contract (see chapter 5) to set and periodically change the net price without consulting the author. Among the factors that publishers consider when doing so are the cost of producing the book, the number of copies that are likely to be sold (particularly during the first year), and the prices being charged for competing books. The latter, until recently, was not an important consideration for textbooks because few instructors appeared to consider price when making adoption decisions. The textbook market now seems to be more price sensitive because of student reaction to high textbook prices.

Expenditures for overhead, researching and preparing the manuscript, and meeting contractual obligations during production also influence book income. Such expenditures can include permission fees (fees you pay for permission to use illustrations and/or text from other publications), postage, fees for having illustrations prepared, and the cost of having photocopies made of research materials and manuscript drafts.

Some expenditures for overhead can actually increase your income from authoring. If you maintain an office in your home *solely for the purpose of authoring books or educational materials* and can convince the IRS that you have a "profit motive" (by having a publishing contract and/or income from it exceeding expenses three out of five years), you ordinarily will be allowed to deduct the expenses resulting from doing so—including a portion of your rent or mortgage payment, electric bill, and heating bill—even if you have an office at your place of employment. The IRS views authoring for which there is a "profit motive" as a business and is likely to accept such an office as being your place of business (see chapter 8).

While it is difficult to estimate the amount of income a book or educational material will generate prior to its publication, the results of a survey that was conducted by the Authors Guild several years ago provides some idea of what is reasonable to expect. The Authors Guild is the principal support organization for book authors in the United States. Ordinarily, a person is not admitted to membership until he or she has had at least one book published. The Guild has approximately 6,500 members, including such "highly successful" authors as James Michener. The average annual income from book writing reported by members of this organization was between $5,000 and $6,000.

Thus far in this discussion, we have assumed that you will not publish and market the book or material yourself. Some academic authors find it advantageous to do both. Self-publishing is more practical than ever before because of the availability of desktop-publishing software and firms—known as service bureaus—that can typeset and produce high quality illustrations from files generated by such software. Further- more, there are now companies that produce books and educational materials for self-publishers that are of the same quality as those sold by book and educational materials publishers. If you self-publish a book or educational material, your income from it will be the money you receive for copies sold minus expenses. The advantages and disadvantages of self-publishing are discussed in chapter 3.

Our focus thus far in this discussion has been on ways that authoring books and educational materials can affect your income directly. There are at least three ways that it can do so indirectly. First, it can result in your receiving a larger merit pay increase than you would have other- wise. Many employers (including colleges and universities) regard the publication of a book as being worthy of such an increase. Second, it can result in your being offered a position at another institution at a higher salary because the book or educational material has enhanced your professional reputation. And third, it can result in your receiving invitations to give lectures or conduct workshops for which you receive an honorarium.

Contributing to Your Field and Enhancing Your Professional Reputation

Extra income isn't the only benefit that you can derive from author- ing an educational book or material. Another is contributing to your field and, as a consequence, having your professional reputation en- hanced. Making a contribution to the field was the benefit mentioned most often by the authors whom I interviewed. Their comments in- cluded the following:

I write books to make a contribution to the profession.

I enjoy knowing that I am helping students across the United States to learn mathematics.

I don't write books primarily to make money. My first objective has been to do a good job of making instructional materials. I've been innovative, had ideas that I thought ought to be used in the classroom. And I have been able to implement them by presenting them in books.

Writing a book is a labor of love. What you're trying to do is to serve the profession by getting better textbooks out there.

The publication of an educational book or material is likely to enhance your reputation at your institution and in your discipline. Comments by the authors whom I interviewed included the following:

There are career benefits. Authoring them can make you a senior professor in your field. For example, I was the senior statistics professor in business administration at my university. Therefore, I was on 20 to 30 doctoral committees all the time. And I was the major professor for at least half a dozen Ph.D. and master's degree students each year.

The professional recognition I get from my department and colleagues is a real plus. It has helped me in terms of promotion and raises. Beyond that there is a certain recognition in the field. My books are advertised. My colleagues in political science come up to me and say they've seen my book.

It is good for the ego to have your name known throughout the country in your field. When persons are familiar with your text or have adopted it, they seek you out at conferences.

I became the president of a 60,000-member professional organization because of my book. It gave me tremendous visibility.

Delaying the Onset of "Burnout"

Another benefit that can come from authoring books and educational materials is delaying the onset of (or possibly even preventing) "burnout." Any job, including teaching, after a while becomes routine. The more routine it becomes, the more likely you are to experience burnout. One way to reduce the likelihood of burnout is by having a second professional activity you can pursue on a daily basis that you both enjoy and find challenging. Authoring can be such an activity. It can be engaged in during any season of the year, in any environment, and the equipment and supplies needed for doing it can be relatively inexpensive. Most of those who do it will at least make enough to pay expenses. In a way, it can be viewed as a form of do-it-yourself psychotherapy—an activity that can make you look forward to getting up in the morning. This is one of the main reasons why I have been authoring textbooks and professional books since the early 1970s and am likely to continue doing so in the future. It also seems to be one of the main reasons some others continue authoring them, judging by comments such as the following:

> It makes my life more interesting.

> I think the major benefit for me is continuing to expand my knowledge and satisfying my curiosity about things I don't know.

Pursuing an Activity You Enjoy

Several of the authors whom I interviewed mentioned that one of the main benefits they derive from authoring textbooks or professional books is having an excuse to write. They enjoy writing. One commented:

> I like writing. . . . It's not difficult for me. If I had to pull hairs and just struggle, struggle, and struggle, I don't think it would be worth it mentally and emotionally because it can wear you down if it takes that much out of you. When I start, I just get more energy. I find myself thinking about it all the time, almost subconsciously, and I just can't wait to get home and get at the yellow pad!

Improving Your Teaching Effectiveness

Authoring a textbook can make you a more effective teacher. This is true, in part, because it forces you to stay current in your field. One of the authors whom I interviewed commented: "Authoring a textbook makes you a much more effective teacher [because] . . . not only are you current, but . . . you have considered the pedagogical questions of what is the most effective way to organize and present material."

POTENTIAL LOSSES

My focus, to this point, has been on ways you can benefit from authoring a book or educational material. Authorship, like all activities, can have a downside. It can, for example, put you at increased risk of experiencing rejection. There are several scenarios under which it can do so. One is that your proposal or manuscript will be rejected. Book proposals rarely are accepted "as is" by the first publisher to which they're submitted. Consequently, you are likely to experience rejection at least once before being awarded a contract. If you attempt to find a publisher after completing a manuscript, you are likely to experience it a number of times, particularly if you submit the completed manuscript rather than a proposal. Most textbook and professional book publishers prefer to take on a project at the proposal and sample chapter stage because they have more control over the final product. An author who has already completed a manuscript is less likely to accept editors' and reviewers' suggestions than he or she would be at the proposal stage. Furthermore, because academic authors usually do not write textbooks, professional books, or scholarly books until they have a publishing contract, if you submit a completed manuscript the editor may assume that it was contracted for and rejected by another publisher. This assumption, of course, is likely to influence how he or she evaluates the manuscript, thereby increasing the likelihood that he or she will reject it. Consequently, if you do complete a manuscript before seeking a publishing contract, do not submit it. Prepare a proposal package and submit it instead. The only exception would be a publisher that does not award contracts from proposals (only from completed, or nearly completed, manuscripts) or one that is aware that you have a manuscript and asks you to submit it.

Another scenario that can lead to your experiencing rejection is if your book sells less well than you hoped. If it is a textbook, it may not be adopted as widely as you expected it to be. Or some of those who adopt it may cease doing so after a semester or two. Another scenario that can lead to your experiencing rejection is if your book receives a "bad" review or is not cited when it should have been.

Experiencing rejection is likely to result—at least momentarily—in a loss of self-esteem and trigger the grieving process. One stage in this process is depression. If you realize why you are depressed, experience it, and then get on with your life, the fact that authorship occasionally causes you to grieve should not outweigh the benefits that you gain from engaging in it.

Another possible contributor to the downside of authoring is the effect that doing so can have on your relationships with colleagues. The following comment by an experienced textbook author is revealing in this regard:

> Your friendships are going to change. . . .When you tell your professional friends that you're going to write a textbook, you will probably lose many of them because of jealousy that you're doing it, fear that you're going to change and you are going to get a big head over it, not quite understanding why you're so preoccupied, and not really supporting it even though outwardly they may say "Oh gee, that's great!" . . . In fact, the ones at school who supported me the most were the cooks and the custodians. When they found out I was writing a book, they thought it was wonderful.

Several factors determine whether these relationships will be harmed. One is how secure your colleagues are professionally. Another is the extent to which you maintain a "high" profile with regard to this activity. If you communicate to your colleagues that you believe you are better than they are because you have written (or have a contract to write) a book, you are likely to have problems. On the other hand, if you maintain a "low" profile and don't talk much about your book, your relationships with them are unlikely to be harmed. The following comment by one of my interviewees relates to this: "I maintain a low profile because of the possibility of jealousy. My colleagues in the math department know very little about my activities beyond the classroom. I just don't want any problems."

If you are an assistant professor and are considering authoring a textbook, you should attempt to determine how members of your department's and college's promotion and tenure committee are likely to react to your doing so. If you are on the faculty of a relatively small teaching-oriented college, writing a textbook is likely to help your case, particularly if it is being used at a large number of institutions. As one interviewee who is a full professor at such a college commented: "At our university authoring a textbook is likely to help your case if you are an assistant professor going for promotion and tenure. We are a medium-size regional university. We are not a high-powered research institution."

On the other hand, if you are on the faculty of a large research-oriented university, their most probable reaction might be such that you would not want to write a textbook before being tenured. According to one interviewee who has been a member of the promotion and tenure committee at such a university, "many professors . . . think that writers of textbooks are writing to make money instead of to advance their discipline. And that makes them feel superior."

One factor that is likely to affect how a promotion and tenure committee will react to your authoring a textbook is your publication record for articles in refereed professional journals. If it is good, they are less likely to react negatively to your authoring a textbook. They also are less likely to do so if you use it as evidence of teaching competence rather than scholarly productivity. If you have authored a textbook based on one of your courses that has been adopted by a large number of colleges, it can be used for making the case that the course is a good one.

Authoring books also can affect other relationships adversely. Those with your spouse, children, and other family members may be particularly vulnerable. Book writing is a solitary activity—one you ordinarily cannot share with members of your family. Consequently, you are almost certain to be spending less time with them. Several interviewees commented on this:

> Your family can undermine your writing efforts without ever saying anything. And the way they undermine it is by making you feel like you're taking time away from them.

> My sister, and my brother, and my parents weren't particularly excited or supportive. I said, "No we can't come home for Christmas. I've got to work on the book. These other chapters are due. I've got to get this done." People who don't write don't understand that you have to meet deadlines.

> We don't happen to have children. If we had children, there would be a big loss for them because they wouldn't have my time.

Furthermore, if your spouse is competing with you and your book is successful, the resulting envy and/or jealousy could have a detrimental effect on your relationship with him or her.

We are becoming increasingly aware that people can become addicted to an activity. Authoring educational books and materials is undoubtedly an activity to which you can become addicted. Authors who remember the writing of their first book and reactions to it as pleasant (for the most part) are likely to write another. Even those who do not remember it in this way may do so. There are several reasons. First, writing can become a part of your daily routine. To complete a book-length manuscript it is necessary to establish and adhere to a writing schedule. After you finish it, you are likely to experience the resulting void in your daily routine as a loss and grieve. As one interviewee commented, "expect the post-partum depression syndrome when you send off the last chapter. The first time I had it, I didn't know what it was. I was just lower than a snake's belly." One way that a person may attempt to cope with the depression associated with grieving is by writing another book to fill the void.

Another reason why someone who does not remember the writing and publication of a first book as being particularly pleasant may write another one is similar to that which causes people to become addicted to gambling. Some people invest heavily in state lottery tickets, bingo, or other forms of gambling because they expect to win eventually. If an author does not "win" with his or her first book, he or she may continue writing them, hoping eventually to do so. Winning in this context could include receiving an amount of royalty income that you regard as substantial, having many adoptions (for a textbook), being invited to conduct workshops, and/or becoming well known and respected in your field.

Some can become so addicted to writing that they will write and submit material for publication that they know isn't good. George Bernard Shaw (the playwright), for example, after turning out some awfully bad stuff in his nineties, is reported to have indicated that he knew the stuff was bad but had become so addicted to writing that he couldn't stop (Krementz, 1996).

I have attempted to present the case here for and against authoring educational books and materials as candidly and objectively as I can. It is not my intention to discourage you from authoring them. The benefits that I have received during the past 25 years from doing so have far outweighed the losses. This appears to be how many experienced authors look upon it, judging by the comments of the ones whom I interviewed and those by others in publications of TAA and the Authors Guild.

3

Choosing a Publisher

If, after weighing the potential benefits and losses, you decide to go ahead with your book or educational material project, your next task is to decide how to publish it. There are two options. You can have a publisher do it or you can publish it yourself. While most authors are likely to choose the first option and only go to the second if they're unable to interest a publisher in the project, their choice may not be the one that is most advantageous for them (e.g., the one that is likely to generate the most income). Possible advantages of the self-publishing option for academic authors are considered elsewhere in this chapter.

THE PUBLISHER OPTION

If you choose the first option, you will have to select a publisher (or publishers) to submit a proposal to. There are several types of book publishers and those of a given type can differ from each other in significant ways. The decision of which publisher (or publishers) to submit a proposal to can affect the likelihood of both your being offered a contract and your book being marketed adequately.

Types of Book Publishers

Trade Book Publishers

These publish fiction and mass-market nonfiction. Their books are sold in community (e.g., shopping mall) bookstores and other retail outlets (e.g., drugstores). Although some of the books they publish appear on class reading lists and are of interest to working professionals, most do not publish textbooks or books intended primarily for professionals in a particular field. Trade book publishers usually prefer to have proposals submitted by literary agents rather than directly by authors. In fact, many of the more prestigious ones are unwilling to consider proposals submitted by authors.

Textbook Publishers

These publish college and/or elementary-high school (designated as *el-hi* or *k–12*) textbooks. If a firm publishes both types, they probably are handled by different divisions. El-hi textbooks are sold directly to schools. College textbooks are distributed either by bookstores owned or leased by the institution or by independent bookstores on or near the campus that specialize in such books. Textbook publishers usually prefer to deal directly with authors. They may, in fact, refuse to consider proposals submitted by an agent.

Most el-hi textbooks today are team rather than individually authored. During the past two decades, the role of the author has been de-emphasized. The names of high-profile people who contributed little or nothing to them often appear on their title pages. Such persons are known as "phantom authors." According to Keedy (1992, p. 2):

> Twenty years ago authors' names were always printed prominently on the covers of textbooks . . . at the el-hi level. Those names have gradually been moved, to the spine, then to the inside and in many cases they have entirely disappeared. It is common today to find only a list of "consultants," rather than authors. Those whose names appear may have little or nothing to do with the writing of the text, the actual writing having been done by development houses or employees of a publisher, many of them with questionable credentials.

Development houses are firms el-hi publishers contract with to develop a whole textbook series or to complete one after the books have been written "in house." In the latter case, they may be asked to write the teacher's editions, workbooks, and/or other ancillary materials (Delbert, 1991).

Although the opportunities for individuals to author texts for the el-hi market are more limited than they are for the college one, they do exist, particularly at the high school level for courses that are not large-enrollment ones or are not taught in the traditional manner. They are particularly likely to be there for teachers who are willing to self-publish (Applebaum, 1988).

Fortunately, the vast majority of college textbooks are not produced by development houses or authored by publishers' employees. College textbook publishing in the United States is an industry with annual sales of over a billion dollars. According to MacDonald (1983): "The college market consists of 12–15 million students enrolled at more than 3,000 two- and four-year colleges and universities. About 300 publishers sell to the college market, though a dozen of them account for 60 percent of all college sales." There is considerable competition among publishers for market share, particularly for the larger, lower-division undergraduate courses (introductory psychology or chemistry or biology, for instance). A publisher may invest well over a million dollars in a text for such a course before the first copy is sold (MacDonald, 1983).

Professional and Academic Book Publishers

These publish specialized books and monographs, intended for academics, working professionals, and professionals in training, that ordinarily would not be used as required textbooks in lower-division undergraduate courses. They usually are sold by the publisher (through direct-mail advertising or advertising in professional publications) or by college bookstores, particularly if they are adopted as texts for upper-division undergraduate or graduate courses. Professional and academic book publishers, like textbook publishers, prefer to negotiate directly with authors.

University Presses

These are major publishers of professional reference books, particularly those intended for academics. Since most major university presses are highly selective about the books they publish, having a book published by one is likely to be viewed by your colleagues as prestigious. If you are an assistant professor, having a book published by a university press would be less likely to be a liability during the "promotion and tenure" process than having one published by any other type. In fact, having a book published by a major university press would almost always be a "plus" during this process.

Another reason a person may choose to have a book published by a university press is to ensure that it remains "in print" for a relatively long time. Textbook and professional book publishers often do not keep books in print once they stop selling. Once a book's sales drop below a certain number per year, it is likely to be declared "out of print." The copies that remain in the warehouse may be offered to the author (usually at low cost), sold to a "remainder" wholesaler, or destroyed. Remaindered books are sold by bookstores, K-Mart, and the like for a fraction of their retail price. Authors do not receive royalties on them. University presses tend to keep books in print longer than other publishers because they have both a weaker profit motive and a stronger scholarly one.

Vanity (Subsidy) Publishers

These publish all types of books. They solicit authors, mostly through direct mail and classified advertisements in magazines. Their books are usually sold (if, in fact, they are sold) directly by them or by the author. They make their money by having authors *subsidize* the publication of their books. As most of the books they publish are unlikely to appeal to anyone except the author's family and friends (therefore, the label "vanity"), these publishers usually do not try very hard to market their books nationally. Also, having a book published by one can damage your reputation because it is well known that they will publish almost anything.

The only type of "respectable" publisher that is likely to ask you to partially subsidize the publication of your book is a university press. You are most likely to be asked to do this—that is, provide an *author subvention*—if your book is one for which the market is very small and grant support for publication expenses is available.

Internet Publishers

This form of book publishing is a relatively recent phenomenon. These publishers publish and market their books on the Internet in electronic form—as downloadable word-processor-compatible files. Some also make books available in printed form (by making printouts of their files). They list the books they publish at their site on the World Wide Web. Ordering is done electronically, with payment usually being made by credit card. A royalty is paid to the author on each copy sold.

The books they publish may or may not be reviewed by external reviewers. One such publisher, when this chapter was written, was ETEXT (etext@etext.net).

How Publishers of a Particular Type of Book Differ from Each Other

A publisher of a particular type of book (e.g., college textbooks) may differ from others of the same type in several ways. One is its size—that is, the number of books it publishes each year. A large one usually publishes more than 50; a medium-sized one between 10 and 50; and a small one fewer than 10 per year (Meyer, 1984).

The size of the publisher that you should seek out depends, in part, on what acquisitions editors are likely to assume—before publication—will be the size of the market for your book. *Acquisitions editors* are the persons at publishing houses to whom book proposals are submitted and with whom contracts are negotiated. If your book is a textbook and they are likely to assume that the market for it is large (e.g., if it is a textbook for an introductory psychology, biology, or math course), you probably would do best financially to seek a contract from a relatively large firm. Large textbook publishers, such as Prentice-Hall, tend to invest most of their marketing resources in books that appear—prior to publication—to have the potential to become "best sellers." A book ordinarily will be viewed as having this potential if its share of the market for a large-enrollment, widely offered course is likely to exceed 20 percent. Large textbook publishers tend to invest relatively little in marketing books that they do not regard—prior to publication—as having this potential. Consequently, some of the books they publish are unlikely to sell as well as they would have if more resources had been invested in marketing them. What we have here can become a self-fulfilling prophecy—that is, because a textbook is not expected to become a "best seller," relatively little is invested in marketing it, which results in relatively few copies being sold. If, however, a textbook does sell many more copies than expected during the first six months following publication, the resources invested in marketing it may (but not necessarily will) be increased.

The difference in marketing investment for a textbook may not be limited to advertising. It also may affect the preparation of the manuscript and the production of the book. If a textbook is thought to have the potential to be a "big" one, a *developmental editor* is likely to be assigned to the author. His or her role is to assist the author in making the book a successful one. The services a developmental editor may provide include obtaining photographs and illustrations, arranging to have parts of the manuscript rewritten to make them more interesting and understandable to undergraduates, and arranging for extensive reviewing of chapters by potential adopters. There may also be a difference in the appearance of the book. Books regarded as having the potential to become "best sellers" are more likely than others to have text printed in several colors and to contain color photographs and drawings. Because textbooks that are given this special treatment tend to be better written and more attractive than they would have been otherwise, the likelihood of their being adopted increases. This difference in quality contributes to the self-fulfilling prophecy referred to previously.

The size of the firm may not be as significant for professional books, scholarly books, and educational materials as it is for textbooks. Very few such books and materials have the potential of selling hundreds of thousands of copies, which often is the case for textbooks for large-enrollment undergraduate courses. However, even with these types of books, an acquisitions editor's assumption prior to publication about the size of the market for a book will influence how much his or her firm is likely to invest in producing and marketing it.

Why would a publisher go to the expense of publishing a book and then do relatively little to advertise or otherwise market it? Judging by letters-to-the-editor and other comments in publications of the Authors Guild and the Text and Academic Authors Association, this question has been perplexing authors for years. Comments that have been made to me by acquisitions editors suggest there could be several reasons. One is the belief that advertising, particularly journal advertising, is unlikely to increase a book's sales significantly. A second is that to be viewed as a "major player" for a discipline a firm has to publish a number of books for students and professionals in it. Merely publishing a few undergraduate textbooks isn't sufficient, even if they are widely adopted. Consequently, acquisitions editors sometimes offer contracts for books they don't expect to be big sellers, ones on which their firm is likely to earn a small profit with a minimal investment of resources. A third is that they are expected to acquire a certain number of books each year. In this regard, an acquisitions editor told me (at a cocktail party after having a few drinks) that in her firm the middle of December is a good time to submit a proposal for a book that is unlikely to be a big seller. If an acquisitions editor hasn't met his or her yearly quota, he or she may be more willing to offer a contract for such a book than would be likely otherwise. And a fourth possible reason is that acquisitions editors really can't predict with a high degree of accuracy which books are likely to become bestsellers. However, if they publish a large number of books, the odds are that at least a few will become bestsellers, particularly if they weed out through the proposal review process (see Chapter 4) those that have little or no chance of becoming one.

If your book is unlikely to be viewed by an acquisitions editor for a large publisher as one that has the potential to become a best seller, you may be better off submitting your proposal to a smaller firm. What for one publisher is a relatively small market, for another is a relatively large one. While a smaller firm probably has fewer resources than a larger one to invest in producing and marketing its books, it may be willing to invest more in producing and marketing your book than would a larger firm. Because a small firm publishes fewer books than does a large one, it is likely to place greater importance on having each book contribute significantly to its "bottom line" than is a large one. Consequently, it is likely to make more of an effort to market books that it views as having limited market potential than is a large one.

Another way that academic book publishers differ from each other is in the fields in which they specialize. Some are "major players" in many fields and others in only a few. You almost always will find it advantageous to submit your proposal to a publisher (or publishers) that already has a "list" in your field. You can identify possible ones in several ways, including scanning bibliographies for your field that include books published during the past five years, checking the listing for your field in *Books in Print,* and checking the directory *Literary Market Place* (published annually by R. R. Bowker Company).

About the only circumstance under which it may not be advantageous to seek a publisher that is established in your field is if you find one that has a good reputation in some other field but likes your proposal and would like to branch out into that field. Such a publisher might be willing to invest more resources in producing and marketing your book than would an established one in your field in order to "test the waters" and/or begin laying a foundation for becoming established.

Writing an Academic Book before Receiving a Contract

It is risky to write a book for which you don't have a publishing contract. The main risk, of course, is that you won't find a publisher. Most academic authors will not write a book without a contract unless they are planning to self-publish it (or are willing to do so if they can't find a publisher) or believe that a publisher is highly likely to offer a contract for it—either after reviewing the entire manuscript or after witnessing the success of a self-published edition. Two of the most successful textbooks in my field—revised editions of which have been published by Prentice Hall for more than 25 years—were initially self-published by their authors. The one that has been in print the longest—*Speech Correction: Principles and Methods* by Dr. Charles Van Riper of Western Michigan University—was self-published in an edition of 500 mimeographed copies in the late 1930s. Dr. Van Riper was refused a contract by Prentice Hall before he self-published it because the acquisitions editor thought that the market was too small. After selling 499 of the copies in less than a year, he sent the 500th to Prentice Hall and received a contract.

Another reason why writing a book, particularly a textbook, before having a publisher is risky is that you may have to do considerable rewriting. Textbook proposals and manuscripts usually are sent to potential adopters for review. If the content and organization are not acceptable to a high percentage of potential adopters, the author will be asked to do what is necessary to make both acceptable. It is easier to do this when a book project is at the proposal stage than after it is written.

As I indicated previously, if you do write a book before receiving a contract, you may have a greater chance of receiving one from an academic book publisher if you submit a proposal with a sample chapter or two rather than an entire manuscript. A publisher that routinely awards contracts for proposals and sample chapters is likely to assume that your manuscript was written for another publisher and rejected. This assumption, of course, would make it less likely that the publisher would give your manuscript serious consideration.

For further information about finding a publisher, see Applebaum (1988), Balkin (1981), Bell (1985), Kozak (1990b), Luey (1987), Meyer (1984), and Powell (1985).

THE SELF-PUBLISHING OPTION

Our focus thus far has been on the option of having a book or educational material published by somebody other than its author. Most academic authors choose this option because they regard it as being the most respectable. They may also choose it because they do not feel qualified to produce and market their book or material and/or do not want to subsidize its publication. Nevertheless, increasing numbers of educational book and material authors are choosing the self-publishing option for at least some of their projects, including ones for which they could get a publishing contract.

Self-publishing is not the same as "vanity" (subsidy) publishing. Authors who self-publish assume the financial and other responsibilities required for production and marketing. For books, these responsibilities include editing the manuscript, preparing camera-ready copy of text and illustrations, printing and binding the book, advertising (marketing) the book, and filling orders for the book. They are likely to contract with others to do some of these tasks. Few academic book publishers, incidentally, use in-house staff for most of these tasks. They employ freelancers to edit manuscripts and do artwork and are likely to contract with other firms to do their typesetting, printing, and binding. Because a self-publishing author can use these same freelancers and firms, a self-published book can be of the same quality as a commercially published one. Self-publishing authors usually publish under the name of a "press" rather than their own name. For books and other materials that I self-publish, I use the imprint Codi Publications.

One difference between self-publishing and "vanity" press publishing is that the former tends to be looked upon as respectable and the latter does not. Vanity press publications, rightly or wrongly, tend to be viewed as low grade. This stigma is not automatically attached to self-published books. In fact, if you self-publish a book under the name of a press (rather than your own name), readers and reviewers are likely to regard it as having been commercially published. The following are books that were initially self-published and are now almost universally regarded as being "respectable": *The Elements of Style* (William Strunk, Jr., and E. B. White); *Familiar Quotations* (John Bartlett); *Robert's Rules of Order* (Henry M. Roberts); *Poor Richard's Almanack* (Benjamin Franklin); and *Huckleberry Finn* (Mark Twain). Self-publishing has become so respectable that in a segment dealing with it on CNN (May 12, 1997), it was revealed that major bookstores—such as Barnes & Noble—are now selling large numbers of self-published ("small press") books.

It isn't unusual, incidentally, for a self-published book to be published later by somebody other than its author. This book, in fact, was originally self-published.

An author may choose to self-publish a book for a number of reasons. Perhaps the most common is that the market for it is too small to interest a publisher, but large enough to be profitable if self-published. Whereas a publisher is likely to have to sell more than 1,000 copies to break even, a self-publisher often can do so from sales of fewer than 100 copies.

Authors sometimes self-publish a book for which they can get a publishing contract. One reason is that they can make more money by doing so. A second reason is that they can have more control over its content and format. A third reason is that it can be kept in print longer. A self-publisher can keep a book in print for as long as it sells any copies or is likely to do so. Some educational books and materials will continue to sell a few copies a year for many years if they are allowed to remain in print. Most academic book publishers will not keep a book in print if it sells only a few copies a year.

Perhaps one of the main reasons why authors self-publish is that doing so enhances their life—makes it more interesting. "Self-publishers, along with a handful of other adults who work with their hands building things they love, are privileged to share the I-made-it-myself elation" (Applebaum & Evans, 1978, p. 141). Also, self-publishers get to interact more directly with readers. "When feedback from readers is favorable, it's a delight; and when it's unfavorable, it may still be instructive" (Applebaum & Evans, 1978, p. 141).

4

Proposals

If you decide to proceed with your book or educational material project and not self-publish it, you will have to prepare a proposal. Actually, you should prepare a proposal even if you are planning to self-publish. It will help you develop a focus (orientation) for the project and organize its content.

Most contracts for textbooks and professional books are awarded on the basis of a proposal and a sample chapter (or chapters). An author who has had several such books published may not be asked to submit sample chapters because his or her writing ability can be judged from previous books. We will focus here on the functions of proposals, their preparation, and the review process to which most are subjected.

FUNCTIONS OF PROPOSALS

A proposal is mainly a marketing (sales) tool. Its primary function is to sell publishing rights to a book or educational material before it is created. If it does what it is intended to do, it will result in the offer of one or more publishing contracts.

Authors, incidentally, sometimes submit a proposal to several publishers at the same time. According to MacDonald (1983), in a pamphlet written for the Association of American Publishers, "There is nothing unethical in submitting a textbook proposal to two or three publishers at the same time, though it is only fair to inform those involved that material is being submitted to more than one house." Although doing so is not unethical, it may not be a good idea because there may be something in the proposal that "turns off" prospective publishers. The advantages and disadvantages of submitting proposals to a number of publishers simultaneously are discussed elsewhere in the chapter.

Some publishers do not award contracts for educational books or materials from proposals; they only do so from a complete manuscript. Nevertheless, it is advantageous to prepare a proposal for such a product, in part, because it can be used to secure a commitment from publishers to give the product "serious consideration" after it is completed.

Proposals can be helpful to authors in ways other than enabling them to obtain publishing contracts. A proposal can help an author decide whether a project is worth doing, and if so, what information to present and how to organize it. An idea for a book or educational material that at first seemed to be a good one may not continue to seem so after being put down on paper. For example, an author may realize after preparing a proposal for a textbook that it does not differ sufficiently enough from the existing textbooks for a course to be widely adopted.

Furthermore, preparing an outline forces you to come up with a *first approximation* of a book's or material's content and organization. Even though the content and organization of most educational books and materials differ somewhat from what was specified in their proposals, they usually do not differ from them by very much. One reason, incidentally, why it is desirable to have them differ little from what is specified in the proposal is a legal one. All publishing contracts contain what is referred to as a "satisfactory manuscript" clause. The clause states that if the publisher finds the book or material to be unsatisfactory in "form and/or content," it can refuse to publish it. An author is in a stronger position to contest such a decision if the form and content specified in the proposal is essentially that in the book or material. The "satisfactory manuscript" clause is discussed further in Chapter 5.

PREPARING A PROPOSAL

Publishers want proposals for educational books and materials to contain particular kinds of information. Although this information is not the same for all publishers, there is certain information that almost all of them expect to find in a proposal. This information is described in this section and illustrated in the sample proposal in Appendix A.

Documenting That There Is an Adequate-Size Market for the Book or Material

Perhaps the most important paragraphs in a proposal are those intended to convince editors and reviewers that there is a sufficiently large market for the book or material and that publishing it *is likely to be profitable*. If you fail to convince them of this, you are unlikely to be offered a contract regardless of how good (important) the project is or how qualified you are to do it. Consequently, in a proposal for a textbook, you should include information about courses for which it could be a required text and the number of institutions that offer such courses. You may also want to include information about the number of students who are likely to be enrolled in them, particularly if this number tends to be relatively large.

If there already are texts available for the course(s) for which your book is intended, you should indicate how yours will differ from them and why instructors are likely to adopt yours based on these differences. You may, in fact, want to do a formal feature-need-benefit analysis for both your book and the competition. A *feature* can only be regarded as being a *benefit* if instructors are likely to conclude that it meets a *need* (Figure 4.1). Obviously, if you fail to document in the proposal that your book provides more benefits than competing ones, acquisitions editors are less likely to conclude that the market for it will be sufficiently large to be profitable.

The acquisitions editor for your field at a publishing house is the person to whom you will submit your proposal and correspond about it.

Figure 4.1
Feature-Need-Benefit Analyses

Feature	Need	Benefit
Career chapter	Course for majors	yes
10 exercises per chapter	25 exercises per chapter	no

He or she is the one who will decide (after consulting with at least one senior editor) whether to offer you a contract. If you are offered a contract and accept it (usually after some negotiation), the acquisitions editor probably will shepherd the project until the final manuscript is accepted and the book is "launched" (i.e., released for production). At some publishing houses, the acquisitions editor's responsibilities don't end with a book being launched. He or she oversees the production process and helps to develop the marketing plan.

To build a case that a market of adequate size exists for your upper-level educational book or material, you should include information about the number of persons who are likely to be interested in the book, the number of college and other libraries (including institutional professional ones) that are likely to purchase it, and the upper-division undergraduate, graduate, and continuing professional education classes for which it would be appropriate as a required or recommended text. You may also want to include information about the market for it outside of the United States (in English or other languages) and professional book clubs for which it may be appropriate.

If there are books "in print" on the same topic, you should indicate how yours will differ from them and why these differences are likely to be regarded by potential purchasers as being *benefits*. You may, in fact, want to do a formal feature-need-benefit analysis for both your book and the competition (figure 4.1).

Documenting Your Competency to Do the Project

Your next task is to convince the editors and reviewers who will be evaluating the proposal that you can write well enough and are sufficiently knowledgeable about the topic to deliver an acceptable (satisfactory) manuscript. Your writing ability will be judged by your proposal and sample chapter(s). If they contain many spelling and/or grammatical errors, the acquisitions editor is likely to assume that the manuscript will also. Furthermore, if some of the information in them is inaccurate or outdated, he or she is likely to question whether you have the knowledge needed to do the project.

Unless there is a good reason for not doing so, include an "About the Author" section in the proposal. Highlight those aspects of your professional experience that support your having the knowledge and experience needed to author the book. If it is a textbook and you have taught the course for which the book is intended, mention this. It would be particularly helpful to do so if you have classroom-tested material you are planning to include. Also, mention any professional experience and publications you have had in the area. Finally, list the associations to which you belong that are relevant to the topic of the book or material. Be certain to mention any specific ways that your expertise has been recognized by them, such as being made a Fellow or being asked to serve on a committee related to the topic of the book or on the editorial board of a relevant association journal.

Description of Content and Organization

After you have established that there is a market for the book and that you have the competence to write it, your next task is to describe its content and organization. This information is communicated through a chapter outline (see Appendix A) and a sample chapter, or chapters. The chapter outline, in addition to its obvious functions, can communicate that "you have thought the project through, that there's a book's worth of material in the idea, and that you have devised the best structure to organize it" (Larsen, 1985, p. 15). The sample chapter (or chapters) provides information about the depth at which material is going to be presented, your points of view and biases, your ability to hold a reader's interest, and the clarity of your writing.

Persons to Whom the Book or Material Is Likely to Appeal

You should specify in the proposal whom the users of the book or material are likely to be—that is, the groups to whom it would be worthwhile to market it. Are they likely to be students, working professionals, or both? The answer could be "both" for a book that is either a textbook for a graduate course or a professional book that contains a significant amount of the material that usually is presented in such a course. Although almost all professional books can be used as recommended or required textbooks for upper-division undergraduate or graduate courses, not all textbooks intended for such courses are likely to appeal to working professionals.

You should describe as concretely as you can the specific segment (niche) of the market to which your book or material is intended to appeal. This issue, for college textbooks, refers to the segment(s) of the department/institution continuum for which a book is intended. At one end of this continuum are research-oriented departments in prestigious universities that offer Ph.D. degrees and attract the cream-of-the-crop students. At the other end are departments in state colleges that do not offer graduate degrees, are not particularly research oriented, and attract students representing a wide range of abilities. It usually is not possible to author a text that will appeal to departments at both ends of the continuum. Those at the research-oriented end tend to adopt books that appear to be written on a "high level" and in which much research is cited. Those at the other end tend to adopt ones that appear to be easy to understand and are packaged in a way that is likely to motivate students to read them. Books intended for this segment, for example, are likely to contain more drawings and photographs than those intended for the other. Thus, in texts intended for the upper end of this continuum, you should attempt to convey the "appearance of being challenging" and in those intended for the other end the "appearance of being approachable."

There are several factors to consider when selecting a segment of the department/institution continuum for which to author a textbook. The first is how competent you feel to author one for each of the various segments. The segment, or segments, for which you are likely to feel most competent to author a textbook is the one, or ones, for which you have taught the course for which the book is intended.

A second factor to consider is the competition—available books that appeal to various segments of the market. If there is no book "in print" that is appropriate for a segment of the market that is large enough to be profitable to publish for and you can convince an acquisitions editor that you have the ability to author one for that segment, you are highly likely to be awarded a contract.

A third factor to consider is the size of the market for the various segments of the continuum. In most fields, the segment at the "lower" end tends to be larger than that at the "upper" end. Although it may be more prestigious to author a book for the upper end of the continuum, the book is likely to generate more income if it is authored for the other end (everything else, of course, being equal).

Perhaps the biggest mistake you can make is to attempt to write a book that will appeal to all segments of a course continuum. Such a book is unlikely to be successful unless there is no other that is appropriate for the course.

It may be necessary to identify the *specific segment* (niche) of the market to which your book or material is likely to appeal even if potential purchasers are working professionals rather than students. It may, for example, appeal primarily to persons who share a particular point of view about the topic. This is particularly likely to be necessary if there are several "schools of thought" about it. The persons who are most likely to read your book or use your material are the ones who either share your point of view or are highly motivated to prove you (or it) wrong.

Information Sources for Establishing the Existence of a Market for the Book or Material

Another decision you will have to make when preparing a proposal for an educational book or material is how you are going to establish that a market (niche) for it exists or can be created. It is particularly important that this be documented adequately if the book deals with a topic (specialty, area, field, approach) about which there are no books currently "in print." There could be several reasons why there are none—the topic may be a relatively new (emerging) one or books dealing with it may not be selling well enough to be kept "in print."

Acquisitions Editors' "Surveys"

There are several sources from which you might be able to get information that you could use to "prove" (document) that the market for your book or material is large enough to publish profitably. One is informal surveys by acquisitions editors of firms that publish in your field. Most acquisitions editors informally survey professors and working professionals about emerging areas and courses for which books are needed. One place they are likely to do so is at their firm's exhibit (booth) at your professional association's national convention. In fact, one reason—perhaps the main one—why acquisitions editors attend such conventions is to identify new niches and acquire new projects. While they probably will be reluctant to share what they have learned about possible publishing opportunities if you approach them directly, they may be willing to do so if you approach them indirectly (e.g., during a friendly conversation at a convention "open house" or "happy hour").

The fact that acquisitions editors attend professional and academic association conventions, in part, to acquire new projects makes this situation a useful one for screening publishers to determine which ones will give your project *serious consideration* at this time. The words "serious consideration" are italicized because they are used by an acquisitions editor to indicate that a project is one in which he or she has some interest and, consequently, the proposal will be subjected to at least the initial stages of his or her firm's evaluation process. However, a project being given "serious consideration" is no guarantee that a contract offer will be forthcoming. Many projects that are given "serious consideration" and begin the evaluation process are rejected before they complete it.

An acquisitions editor who is unwilling to give your project serious consideration when you initially contact him or her may be willing to do so at some future time. There could be several reasons for this. One is that the market needs remain unchanged, but the acquisitions editor gets new information that makes your project appear more viable than it did initially. Another possible reason is that the market needs are changing. A niche has been created that your project could fill. A third possibility is a change in the status of the publisher's "list." At the time your proposal is received, the publisher may have a similar book "in print," "in press," or "in process." Sales of an existing book may falter or one "in process" may not be completed. Either scenario could result in serious consideration being given to your proposal.

Do not assume because one acquisitions editor for a firm is unwilling to give your project serious consideration that another employed by that firm will also be unwilling to. Acquisitions editors for many educational/professional book and material publishers change frequently. One of the textbook authors whom I interviewed stated that "in the 28 years that I have been an author for McGraw-Hill, I have never had the same acquisitions editor for more than a 3-year period." During the 25 years that I have been authoring books for the college division of Simon & Schuster (S & S), I have had at least a dozen acquisitions editors. There have been two instances in which an acquisitions editor for S & S refused to give serious consideration to a project I proposed and the one who replaced him or her was willing to do so. In both instances, incidentally, I was offered a contract by the "replacement" acquisitions editor. A publisher's refusal to give serious consideration to a project can be interpreted as being merely a lack of interest in the project by a *particular* acquisitions editor *at the time* the refusal was issued. Consequently, the reluctance of a publisher to give a project serious consideration is not necessarily "engraved in stone." The following advice from an acquisitions editor whom I interviewed seems pertinent here: "I would suggest that authors resubmit proposals. As with résumés, it is a good idea to keep proposals current. . . . This is no guarantee of present or future acceptance . . . but your proposal stands more of a chance of acceptance sitting in my filing cabinet than it does sitting in yours."

Recent Changes in Your Field

Another possible source of evidence for documenting that there is a market for your book or material is recent changes (developments) in your field. If there have recently been significant changes (developments) in your field, there may be a market for textbooks that include information about them. Since such changes are likely to be of interest to working professionals—particularly if they have practical implications—there could also be a market for a professional book that deals with them, particularly one that could serve as a textbook for upper-division undergraduate or graduate courses. Consequently, if there are no books "in print" that describe these changes (developments) and the one that you are proposing does, you can use this information to argue that there is likely to be a market for your book.

I used this strategy to support a proposal for a textbook for the stuttering course that all students majoring in speech-language pathology are required to take. There were at least a dozen texts for the course, all of which dealt exclusively, or almost exclusively, with stuttering. A recent trend in the field had been an increasing interest in disorders, other than stuttering, that can have a detrimental effect on a person's speech fluency. I argued that the book I was proposing—*Stuttering and Other Fluency Disorders*—would be competitive because it would be the only one that would provide students with the information they need to manage all fluency disorders, not just stuttering. The acquisitions editor and reviewers bought my argument and a second edition was published recently.

The publication of a book that would be appropriate to use as a text for a course that does not exist can serve as a catalyst for the course being created—that is, the book can create the course. The development of courses on microcomputer applications for specific fields illustrates this. By the mid-1980s, professionals in many fields had begun using microcomputers routinely for such applications as word processing, database management, number crunching, teaching, and communication. Some persons in these fields thought there was a need to incorporate discipline-specific material about microcomputer applications in training programs for them and books were written that could be used for this purpose as well as for informing working professionals about this technology. Their presence served as a catalyst for microcomputer courses being introduced into the curriculum of many disciplines, including my own (speech-language pathology).

It is risky to author a textbook for a course in an emerging area. Only a few departments may add the course during the first few years following its publication and, consequently, the number of copies sold may not be large enough to keep the book "in print." If courses for which the book is appropriate develop more than a few years after its publication, the book may still not sell well (assuming that it is still "in print") because the literature in emerging areas tends to expand rapidly and, consequently, the review of it in the book is likely to be out-of-date. Furthermore, the book's acquisitions editor probably will be unable to get authorization from his or her senior editor to publish a new updated edition because sales of the first edition were too low. Two of the four times that I authored a textbook for a course in an emerging area, only a few departments added the course during the first three years following its publication.

Another reason why it is risky to author a textbook for an emerging area is that others in your discipline may also be doing so. Consequently, even if a number of departments do add a course for which the book is appropriate during the first few years following its publication, the book would be unlikely to be adopted by all of them. Although the size of the market may be adequate for one book, it may not be so for several. Furthermore, because you will be unlikely to have information about the books with which yours will have to compete while you are writing it, you will be unable to judge how well yours is likely to compete with them. I am not trying to discourage you from authoring a book for an emerging area. The benefits from doing so to both income and reputation can be substantial. However, be aware of the risks, particularly if the book is unlikely to sell well to working professionals.

Other Information Sources

There are several other ways that you may be able to document the existence of a market for your project. If the project is a textbook, one approach that's worth considering is surveying persons who teach a course for which the book would be appropriate about the need for a text of the type you have in mind. Surveys could also be used to document the need (and consequently, a market) for other types of educational and professional books and materials.

Another way you may be able to establish that your project is viable is by documenting the existence of similar products for related fields. If, for example, there were books on microcomputer applications for a number of health-related fields but not speech-language pathology, you could argue that there should also be a market for one in speech-language pathology. Incidentally, I used this argument successfully in a proposal that I circulated for such a book during the mid-1980s.

Guidelines for Preparing Proposals

Perhaps the best way to summarize what should be in a proposal for a textbook or other educational book or material is by furnishing a representative set of guidelines. One that was developed by a large publisher of college textbooks is reproduced below. Much of it is also applicable for proposals for educational books and materials other than textbooks. The words in square brackets were added by me to make these guidelines more relevant for such projects.

I. **The Prospectus and Outline.** The prospectus and outline provide a general frame of reference for your work. It is your book's story.

  A. The Book

    1. *Brief description:* In one or two paragraphs describe the work, its approach, and your purpose in writing such a text [or professional book].

    2. *Outstanding features:* List briefly what you consider to be outstanding or unique features of the work.

    3. *Pedagogical features:* Will the book include summaries, examples, cases, questions, problems, and so forth?

    4. *Supplements:* Do you plan to provide supplementary material such as a teacher's manual, study guide, lab manual, solution's manual, software, or other?

    5. *Level:* For whom is the book intended and what is the level? What are the prerequisites, if any?

    6. Has the material been class-tested? If not, will it be?

  B. Your Background

    1. Please provide a description of your background, relevant professional activities, number of times you have taught this course [if it is a textbook], and other writing experiences.

    2. Please attach a copy of your vita.

       3. Do you have other writing plans when this project is complete?

  C. The Competition

      1. *Top three books in the field:* How does your book compare and/or contrast with them? Please discuss each competing book in a separate paragraph. Please include author, title, publisher, publication date, length, and price (if known).

      2. Please focus on comparing topical coverage, organization, level, writing style, art program, pedagogy, and any other relevant similarities and differences between your project and the competing books.

      3. *Be frank:* This information is written for reviewers, providing them with a comparative framework, and should accurately reflect your views.

      4. Are you aware of any similar works in progress but [that are still] unpublished?

  D. The Market

      1. What is the primary course [or professional group] for which the book is intended? What other courses [or professional groups] would it serve? Would it be appropriate for international, high school, or trade markets?

      2. What is your expectation of the size of the market?

      3. If you have done any market research of your own, we would appreciate receiving a brief summary of your findings.

  E. The Outline

      1. The outline provides an overview of the entire work: It is the road map guiding both the reviewer and the publisher along your specific point of view.

      2. Chapter heads should be followed by subheads that explain the content at a greater level of detail.

      3. Paragraphs should be used as needed to clarify the outline.

      4. If revision of the sample material is requested, always provide a revised outline.

II. The Sample Chapters. The sample chapters should illustrate the strongest and most distinctive aspects of your work.

A. It is best to submit three chapters. Two chapters leave the reviewer in doubt and the entire manuscript, while useful, tends to overwhelm the reviewer.

B. Selected chapters should include those that best represent your work's basic idea, its quality, and its distinctive features. They should not include the introductory chapter, nor do they necessarily have to be in sequence.

C. The selected material does not need any illustration other than a rough pencil sketch; remember that your peers are the readers and will quickly understand a brief suggestion for an illustration. At the same time it is crucial to have the suggested illustrations integrated with the manuscript.

D. Prepare the material carefully. If the manuscript is full of typographical or grammatical errors, the reviewers' attention will be diverted from the more important consideration of content.

E. If your manuscript features problems or exercises, please include some samples.

III. **Additional Information.** A few final pieces of information to round out the proposal.

A. What schedule of completion do you have in mind for your book?

B. What will be the approximate length of your work? Please state whether your estimate is based on book or manuscript pages. If dealing in manuscript pages, please describe in terms of 8½" × 11" double-spaced pages.

C. What kind of art program is needed for your book? What is the estimated number of line drawings and photographs? (Please look at competing books for a frame of reference.) Can you prepare the line drawings in camera-ready form?

D. Is the manuscript being prepared on word-processing equipment? Could your manuscript be submitted in camera-ready form? Some manuscripts can be electronically typeset directly from disk or tape, so please describe the equipment you are using.

E. Please list the names and affiliations of some qualified reviewers who could be asked to critique the work.

One point mentioned in these guidelines (II.A) is particularly important—not submitting the entire manuscript. As I have indicated elsewhere, since textbook and professional authors usually do not write books without a contract, if you submit a book the acquisitions editor is likely to assume that it was rejected by the publisher who had it under contract. This could cause the acquisitions editor to look upon the project less favorably than he or she would have otherwise done.

For further information about preparing proposals, see Herman and Adams (1993) and Larsen (1985). While the focus of both books is on proposals for trade books, much of the information in them is relevant for proposals for academic books. The Herman and Adams book is particularly helpful because it includes 10 sample proposals that sold, with comments about why each section in them was crafted as it was.

If a project for which you are preparing a proposal is a textbook, you may find some of the material in Appendixes D and F useful. Appendix D contains information gleaned from interviews with undergraduate students about textbook features that they do and don't find helpful. Appendix F contains a list of characteristics that successful textbooks appear to share.

SUBMITTING THE PROPOSAL

You may submit the proposal to a number of publishers simultaneously or to one publisher at a time. The main advantage that the multiple, simultaneous submissions strategy has over the sequential submission strategy is that you are likely to find a publisher sooner *if there is nothing seriously wrong with your proposal*. However, if there is something seriously wrong with the proposal, you are less likely to find a publisher using this strategy than you are using the other. With the sequential strategy, you can use the acquisitions editor's and reviewers' comments to improve the proposal, thereby bettering the odds of interesting the next publisher to which you submit it. Although it may take a little longer to find a publisher using this strategy, the likelihood of your eventually finding one is greater than if the simultaneous submissions strategy is used.

While the simultaneous submissions strategy is risky, it can result in your being able to negotiate a better contract, assuming, of course, that more than one publisher is interested in the book. Through the bidding process, you may receive a higher royalty rate and/or a larger advance than you would have otherwise. Also, you should be in a better position to negotiate in the deletion or modification of "undesirable" clauses (see Chapter 5).

If your proposal is for a textbook, it may be worthwhile to submit it to a publisher who already has a book for the course, particularly if the publisher is a large one. Some large firms publish more than one text for a course, particularly if the course is an undergraduate one that has large enrollments and is offered by many colleges and universities. It would be important to indicate in the proposal why your book should appeal to instructors who are unlikely to adopt the firm's other text(s)—that is, why publishing your book is likely to increase their market share for the course. The main disadvantage of having your book published by such a firm is that it may not be marketed as aggressively as it would if it were the publisher's only book for the course.

Most acquisitions editors for educational and professional book and material publishers have proposals reviewed externally before making a publishing recommendation to their senior editor. For a project that is not a textbook, the reviewers are likely to be two or three working professionals and/or academics who are knowledgeable about the field. And for a textbook, they are likely to be two or three persons who teach a course for which the book would be appropriate. The author may be given an opportunity to respond to negative comments in the reviews before a decision is made.

As I have previously indicated, the time of year you submit a proposal may influence your likelihood of being offered a contract. This is particularly apt to be the case for proposals that acquisitions editors regard as good but lacking the potential to be big money makers. At a recent TAA convention, over cocktails, an acquisitions editor told me that the middle of December would be a particularly good time to submit such a proposal to her publisher. The month would be different if a publisher's fiscal year did not correspond to the calendar year. The reason is that the acquisitions editors for at least some publishers are expected to acquire a certain number of projects a year. If it is getting close to the end of the fiscal year and they haven't acquired their quota, they may be more highly motivated to offer a contract for such a project than they would be otherwise. There is no reason to believe that they would be less interested in acquiring a project submitted at this time than they would be otherwise. Consequently, if your project is one that acquisitions editors are unlikely to regard as being a "cash cow" and you can delay submitting the proposal until the middle of the last month of a publisher's fiscal year, it may be worthwhile doing so.

Traditionally, proposals have been submitted directly to publishers, usually by mail. An alternative way to submit them was suggested in a presentation at a recent TAA convention. You create a home page on the World Wide Web and attach your proposal(s) to it. You then send query letters to publishers in which you briefly describe the project and give the address of your Web home page. Publishers who want to give serious consideration to the proposal can download it. This method of submission would have at least two advantages over the traditional one. First, it would be less expensive—particularly if you already had a Web home page—because your expenditures for postage and duplicating would be lower. And second, it would be more "attention getting" because of its novelty.

BECOMING A CO-AUTHOR OF ANOTHER AUTHOR'S BOOK OR MATERIAL

Your proposal can be rejected by a publisher and you can still end up receiving a contract from the firm. This happened to one of the authors whom I interviewed: "I actually wrote a proposal for a physiology book. . . . As it turned out, the book I ended up working on wasn't the book I wrote the proposal for. The proposal got me a job as a co-author on an anatomy and physiology book." This is most likely to occur if an author is unable or unwilling to revise a book and the publisher wants a new edition. This sometimes happens after an author retires. Most publishing contracts give the publisher the right to add a co-author if doing so is necessary to keep a book "in print" (see Chapter 5).

Rather than developing a proposal for your own project, you may want to consider proposing that you would like to be a co-author of future editions of an existing book or material, particularly one that has been "in print" for many years and is highly respected by persons in your field. Such a proposal could be made to the present author or co-authors, to their heirs if he, she, or they are deceased, or to the publisher if the author or one of the co-authors has refused to do the revision needed for a new edition. An author who is about to retire or who has retired recently is particularly likely to be seeking such a co-author. Someone who is no longer interested in revising a book may want to take on a co-author because he or she will receive some royalty income from the revised edition, regardless of whether he or she contributes to revising it.

It would be risky to enter into this type of co-authoring arrangement without legal counsel. There are many potential problems with any such arrangement, and perhaps even more with the assumption of property already published. It's to everyone's advantage to have all details spelled out *in writing* before any work is done. Some of the issues that should be dealt with in such a joint collaboration agreement are indicated in Chapter 5.

5

Negotiating a Publishing Contract and a Joint Collaboration Agreement

If all goes well and you are not self-publishing, you will be offered a publishing contract for your project. The contract, itself, will be either a printed form to which information relevant to your project has been added or a document that was printed by a computer. It will consist of standard ("boiler plate") clauses that were drafted by the publisher's attorneys. Your "gut reaction" after receiving the contract is likely to be to sign and return it immediately—before the acquisitions editor has a chance to change his or her mind. As one of my interviewees remarked, "I was so thrilled to get my first contract, I'd have signed anything."

One reason why academic book authors may not attempt to negotiate their book publishing contracts is that they don't think of themselves as owning and operating a small business. In the view of the IRS and other government entities, they are as much a business as is their publisher. Rather than thinking of their book writing as a product that they are producing for which they should be paid, they think of it as being similar to the writing they do for professional journals for which they are not paid. Few, if any, of us negotiate publishing rights for articles that we write for professional journals. Consequently, if you view academic book writing in the same manner, it is not surprising that you wouldn't attempt to negotiate a book-publishing contract.

Some authors who accept the publishing contract for their first project as is (or nearly so) regret later having done so. The following excerpts from interviews with two authors are revealing in this regard:

> What mistakes did we make? We signed a contract that tied us to one publisher for life, that made it possible for the publisher not to reissue the book and to prevent us taking it to another publisher. The contract probably violates the Thirteenth Amendment.

> I just signed my first contract. I knew nothing and I didn't think that I should know anything. But as I went on I became aware of a lot of things I should negotiate. Surprisingly, some publishers went along with a lot of the stuff I've asked for. For example, the competition clause. One publisher said "No, we will not cross that out." So I said, "Fine, good-bye." I went to another publisher and they agreed to cross it out.

Some of the authors whom I interviewed reported that they accepted the contract for their first project "as is" and do not have regrets about having done so. The project in most cases was either a professional or a scholarly book. They appeared to have confidence in the integrity of the publisher and/or they stated that their primary motivation for writing the book was not to supplement their income. The following are representative of their comments:

> What I did was rely on the integrity of the people I was working with. I took their word for what is the standard and since I was interested in getting the book published, I was willing to sign what they called a standard contract. My motivation was not primarily financial and it never has been particularly financially rewarding.

> I always took the attitude that the publishers were businessmen who were honest and sincere, and I could trust them and they would trust me. Therefore, I never really questioned contracts. I did ask sometimes about the royalties, but I was always satisfied with what they told me.

All publishing contracts—even printed ones—are negotiable to some degree. As Michael Lennie, an attorney who specializes in negotiating them, stated: "An offer [of a contract] is an invitation to dicker. A contract is an agreement. An agreement takes two persons. Publishers do not expect you to sign their standard contract as is. Everything in the contract is negotiable. It is merely their wish list."

The degree to which a publishing contract is negotiable is a function, in part, of how badly a publisher wants to publish a project and how badly an author wants a publisher to publish it. *Publishers usually are willing to negotiate more clauses in contracts for textbooks for large-enrollment undergraduate courses than they are those in contracts for scholarly books that are unlikely to be big money makers.* However, publishers are almost always willing to negotiate at least a few of the clauses in contracts for books that are unlikely to be "cash cows" if they are really interested in publishing them.

If you are going to try to negotiate some of the clauses in a publishing contract, you have to prioritize the modifications that you want to have made to them. That is, you have to decide which of them are so important to you that you are willing to "walk away from the table"—not sign the contract—if they are not made. A "walk away" clause for me has always been the one that gives the publisher an automatic option on my next book.

Standard publishing contracts are drafted by publishers' attorneys and tend to favor the publisher. However, as I have already indicated, most publishers, *if asked*, will be willing to negotiate some of the clauses. We will consider in this chapter the clauses in the standard publishing contract and how some might be modified to make the agreement more of a win-win one.

The type of agreement (contract) that we have discussed thus far is between an author, or a group of co-authors, and a publisher. If a project is being authored by more than one person, its co-authors should have a contract with each other—a joint collaboration agreement—in addition to the one that they have with the publisher. There are some suggestions at the end of this chapter for issues to deal with in a joint collaboration agreement.

NEGOTIATING A PUBLISHING CONTRACT

Almost all publishing contracts for textbooks and professional books are negotiated by their authors. This differs from contracts for trade books, which usually are negotiated by a literary agent. The agent receives between 10 and 15 percent of the advance and royalties from the book for doing so. While an agent who is experienced in negotiating textbook and other educational and professional book and material contracts may be able to negotiate a more advantageous one than can an author, there are only a small number of agents who are experienced in negotiating contracts for such projects. Information about them can be obtained from the Text and Academic Authors Association.

If you don't want to do your own negotiating, there is an alternative to having an agent do it. You can have it done by an attorney knowledgeable about publishing. A list of attorneys nationwide who are experienced in negotiating contracts can be obtained from the Text and Academic Authors Association. The cost of retaining an attorney for this purpose tends to be most justifiable for books that have the potential to generate considerable income, such as ones for large-enrollment undergraduate courses.

Some academic authors who negotiate their own contracts have them examined (vetted) by an attorney who specializes in the law of intellectual property (copyright and patent laws) before signing. They do this to make certain that they are not relinquishing rights it would be disadvantageous for them to relinquish or taking on obligations it would be disadvantageous for them to assume. They use the advice they receive from the attorney to negotiate further before signing. The Text and Academic Authors Association and/or your state bar association can provide a referral.

There are a group of clauses that appear in almost all publishing contracts (agreements) for educational and professional books and materials. The implication of each of these clauses is described here, along with suggestions for negotiating some of them. As I have indicated previously, the extent to which you are likely to be able to negotiate changes to these clauses will be determined in large part by how strongly motivated the acquisitions editor is to acquire the project. You should be able to negotiate changes to at least a few of them, even if the acquisitions editor's motivation to acquire the project is relatively low.

Parties to the Agreement

The publisher and the author(s) are clearly identified.

Date of the Agreement

This probably will be the date when the contract was drawn up rather than the one when you were told you would be receiving it. This date is used in correspondence to help identify the contract.

Title, Length, and Delivery Date of the Manuscript

The title indicated may be the actual one or, if a decision has not been made on the title, a "working" one that specifies the book's subject matter.

The length of the manuscript may be specified in words or pages. It usually is based on the estimate given in the proposal. It is better to err on the low side than on the high one. A publisher is more likely to claim that a manuscript is not "satisfactory" if its length is longer than the estimate rather than shorter. Of course, if its length is considerably shorter than the estimate, it may not be possible for the publisher to charge the price it projected when determining whether the project was economically viable and, consequently, it may no longer be so.

The contract will specify a date by which the final manuscript and supporting materials (e.g., instructor's manuals and copyright permissions) are to be delivered. If they aren't delivered by this date, the publisher can cancel the contract and demand that the advance be returned. If the acquisitions editor remains interested in the project, he or she is likely to give the author additional time. Why take chances? Make your estimate realistic, perhaps a little on the high side. Few publishers will object if you deliver the manuscript and supporting materials early.

Grant of Rights

When you sign a publishing contract for a book or material, you transfer at least some of your rights as an author (ones you are given by the Copyright Act of 1976 and subsequent modifications and court decisions) to the publisher for a period of time in exchange for publication and, in most cases, royalty income. It is important that this period not be permitted to extend beyond that when the book or material goes "out of print." You own the copyright on your book or material before signing a publishing contract, whether or not you formally register it with the Copyright Office at the Library of Congress. According to present U.S. copyright law, copyright protection for your work extends until 50 years after your death. As your work is unlikely to remain "in print" for this length of time, the rights you transfer to a publisher should eventually revert to you or to your heirs. Even if much of the material in it is out of date when it goes "out of print," the title, the organization, and some of the material in it may still have the potential (if exploited) to generate income for you or your heirs. The following experience, reported by one of the authors whom I interviewed, illustrates how this could happen:

> The family was involved in the decision regarding whether I would
> be selected to revise the book. A number of years had gone by without a new edition. The book was authored by the husband who was
> an academic, with a fair amount of assistance from the wife who was
> not an academic. The husband had passed away. Since he was the
> primary author, this is the reason they were searching for a new
> one. But the wife was still involved, still very much feeling as
> though it were their book and wanted to have a say in who was selected. One of their major concerns, of course, was that writing
> style be compatible, because they didn't want a new book. They
> simply wanted a revision of that book. The children were also involved because they were heirs of the estate. A couple of the children were attorneys so they were very much involved in the
> contract negotiation.

Another way that an "out of print" book or material can generate income for you is by selling it to another publisher. I have sold revised editions of two "out of print" books to other publishers. Of course before you can do this, the rights that you transferred to the publisher must revert to you.

It is crucial that all publishing contracts contain a *copyright reversion clause* for the reasons that I have indicated. Such a clause states that the copyright will be returned to you or your heirs, for either no charge or a payment of one dollar, when the book goes "out of print" or a revision is not requested after a specified number of years (e.g., three) following publication.

You may also want to specify other circumstances under which the rights you transferred to the publisher will revert to you. One is if the publisher does not accept or reject the manuscript in writing within a specified number of days (e.g., 90) after the time of submission. Another is if the publisher does not publish the book within a certain number of months after acceptance of the manuscript. Although this number will vary depending on the length and complexity of the manuscript, it should not exceed 18 months. The following comment by an author I interviewed illustrates why such a stipulation may be needed:

> What I've got now is a contract I've signed for a book on political
> theory. The manuscript has been sitting for about two years with an
> editor who has done nothing. The reviews have been favorable, but

she says they want more contextual analysis. When I try to pin her down as to what that means, I don't get much of an answer. So they've never said the manuscript is unsatisfactory. They've simply not proceeded to put it into production.

A publisher may do this (i.e., delay publication) to keep your book from competing with one that it either has published or has in preparation. This is particularly likely to occur if your publisher is sold to another publisher that already has "in print" or in preparation one or more books for the course for which your book is intended. This type of merger has become quite common in recent years.

What if you don't have a clause in your contract that requires your publisher to indicate acceptance or rejection of your manuscript within a certain number of days following receipt and to publish it by a certain number of months following acceptance? What if you then encounter this situation? You may be able to get your publisher to revert the rights to you by arguing that it is in its interest to do so. According to Michael Lennie—an attorney who specializes in publishing law—in a presentation at the 1997 Text and Academic Authors Association convention:

> From the publisher's perspective, it mitigates damages the publisher might otherwise be liable for. That is, if the author has a cause of action against the publisher for breach of the agreement to publish, the author has a duty to "mitigate" his or her damages. The only way the author can do this is to seek publication of the Work by another publisher. This, of course, requires reversion of rights. Also, the publisher is subject to criticism—if not liability—for bottling up a competing work it does not intend to publish. In short, the publisher should revert the rights to the author so long as the author is willing to satisfy his or her contractual obligation to repay advances from the "first proceeds" generated by publication of the book by a new publisher.

As I have indicated previously, you own the copyright for your book or material before signing a publishing contract. The copyright is composed of a number of rights. In this clause you agree to transfer (grant) most—if not all—of them to the publisher. By so doing you grant the publisher the exclusive right to publish and sell your book or material until 50 years after your death in all countries, in all languages, and in all media (including electronic media); to sell this right—in whole or part—to another publisher without your permission; and to copyright the book or material in the publisher's name (rather than yours).

About the only change pertaining to the transfer of rights that an academic author may try to negotiate is having the work copyrighted in his or her name rather than the publisher's. Some publishers will agree to do this. However, having this done is essentially meaningless because the author has transferred to the publisher all of the rights to the work that copyright law has granted him or her.

Authors who are represented by a literary agent may not sell these rights as a totality. They may, for example, grant a publisher the right to sell copies of a book in a particular country or a particular language. Or they may grant a book club the right to print and distribute a specified number of copies to its members.

If an author is unagented (as almost all academic authors are) and sells the rights to his or her work as a totality, the publisher will act as his or her agent for the sale of translation, book club, and other publishing (reproduction) rights. The amount a publisher is likely to charge for doing so is 50 percent of the money received. It occasionally is possible to negotiate for a split that is more favorable to the author, for example, a 60–40 split.

Royalties, Advances, and Payments

This clause specifies the royalty percentage(s) and how the royalty will be paid. A royalty percentage may be printed on the contract. Even if one is printed on it, the percentage usually is negotiable. Many first-time authors don't realize this and accept the printed royalty percentage. Royalty percentages for educational and professional books and materials range from 5 to 18 percent, with most being between 10 and 15 percent.

Most publishers of academic and professional books and materials base their royalties on cash received (net income) rather than on the retail price of the work. If your royalty is based on net income, make certain that net is defined in the contract as the cash the publisher receives from sales of the work. Otherwise, the publisher could deduct expenses such as shipping costs and production costs to arrive at net.

Some publishing contracts contain a paragraph that specifies the size of the advance and how it will be paid. An advance is a loan the publisher makes the author that is *usually* interest free. It is repaid from royalties. The word "usually" is added because if the author does not deliver a manuscript that the publisher deems to be "satisfactory," the author usually will be required to return the advance, possibly with interest. If the manuscript is published and sales of the work do not result in sufficient royalties to repay the advance, the author usually is not required to pay the publisher the difference between what the work earned and what is owed.

Don't assume that a publisher will not give an advance if it isn't mentioned in the contract. Many publishers that don't mention an advance in their contracts will give one if asked to do so assertively—particularly if the author indicates that he or she is aware it is customary to give one. The clause specifying the amount of the advance and how it is to be paid will appear on an addendum page (rider) to the contract.

The size of the advance depends, in part, on how badly the publisher wants the work. Most advances for educational and professional books and materials appear to be in the $500 to $5,000 range. It is desirable to get as large an advance as possible because it "guarantees" your receiving some income from the work. Another possible benefit you may gain from a large advance is increased motivation for the publisher to aggressively market your book or material.

You are unlikely to be offered an advance that is larger than the predicted first-year royalties for the work. Consequently, if your work is a book—such as a specialized scholarly one—that is published by a university press and unlikely to sell many copies during the first year following publication, you may be offered a very small advance or none at all.

If the advance is relatively small, ask to have it made payable on signing the contract. Otherwise, have it made payable in two installments—half on signing the contract and half on delivery of the manuscript. If the advance is relatively large (more than $5,000), try for two installments but you may have to settle for more, for example, one-third on signing, one-third after delivery of the first half of the manuscript, and one-third after delivery of the remainder of the manuscript.

Publishers occasionally, if asked, will give an author a grant to cover a specific expense (e.g., preparing illustrations) that does not have to be repaid from royalty income. The following language from the Text and Academic Authors Association's "Guide to Contracts for Publishing Textbooks" may be used for this purpose: "When this contract is signed by both parties, the Publisher will pay the Author a non-refundable grant of [insert amount of money] to defray the following expenses: [insert expenses and amounts]." An academic author is most likely to be given one for a project that is a text for a large-enrollment undergraduate course.

Most publishing contracts specify that royalties and rights income will be paid either once or twice a year. This may be negotiable. You may want to negotiate, for example, to have income from rights sales paid to you within 30 days of receipt by the publisher.

Submission Clause

This clause specifies how to submit your manuscript—that is, whether to do so on sheets of paper, as files on a computer disk, or both. Some publishers typeset by rekeyboarding copyedited manuscripts and others by inserting typesetting commands into word-processor files supplied by the author. Most now do the latter. This clause also specifies the number of printed copies to submit. A publisher that does not intend to typeset directly from the author's word-processor files usually will specify that two copies be submitted. You should, of course, also make a copy of the manuscript for your own use.

"Satisfactory Manuscript" Clause

All publishing contracts contain an escape clause for the publisher (which most authors' organizations refer to as the "satisfactory manuscript" clause). It states that the manuscript must be *acceptable to the publisher in form, style, and content*. There usually are no guidelines in the contract for judging whether a manuscript is satisfactory in these ways. Consequently, a publisher can declare any manuscript unsatisfactory, refuse to publish it, and demand that the advance be returned (possibly with interest).

A publisher may claim that a manuscript is unsatisfactory even if it really isn't. For example, a book may have been published during the period between the signing of the contract and the delivery of the manuscript that filled the niche. Consequently, the publisher no longer considers the book to be one that is likely to be profitable and uses the clause to escape its contractual obligations. Or the publisher may receive another proposal for a book to fill the niche during the period between the signing of the contract and delivery of the manuscript that the acquisitions editor considers more likely to be profitable. A third possibility is that the publisher obtained a book to fill the niche between the signing of the contract and the delivery of the manuscript by acquiring another publisher's books in your field. Such transfer of books from one publisher to another is not uncommon (in fact, this is how my

Prentice-Hall books became Allyn & Bacon books). And a fourth possibility is that there was a change in acquisitions editors and the new one either didn't like the project or didn't view it as having the potential to be profitable. One of my interviewees reported that he had the satisfactory manuscript clause applied for this reason: "A new group came in—new editors—and they wanted to have a whole new vision of the future. I just took the book elsewhere."

It has been argued by spokespersons for both the Authors Guild and the Text and Academic Authors Association that this clause (particularly if it does not include a provision for arbitration) is unfair because it allows the publisher to escape from contractual obligations but not the author—that is, the author is not free after the manuscript is completed to negotiate for a better offer from another publisher.

This clause, in effect, means that a publishing contract at the proposal stage is not binding, but it is advantageous nevertheless to have one for several reasons. First, your colleagues and administrators are more likely to regard your authoring activities as being worthy of support (e.g., your being given a reduced teaching load) if your book is being written under contract to a publisher. Second, having a contract makes it more likely that your book will be published. Third, the manuscript (particularly if it is for a textbook) is likely to require less rewriting if the acquisitions editor's expectations (concerning content, structure, writing style, length, etc.) are known before it is written. And finally, you can use the advance (assuming you receive one) for paying at least some of your manuscript-preparation expenses as well as for proving to the IRS that you have a "profit motive" (see Chapter 8).

One way to cope with this clause is by having a paragraph added to the contract similar to the following one, which states that if the publisher declares the manuscript to be unsatisfactory and the author challenges this decision, both parties agree to have the matter arbitrated by a member of the American Arbitration Association.

> In the event of disputes or disagreements arising from this agreement, both Author and Publisher consent to settle such disputes under the rules and auspices of the American Arbitration Association, and to abide by its binding judgment. Such judgment may be entered in the highest court of the form, state or federal, having jurisdiction thereof. If, however, there is pending litigation related to the issue, either Author or Publisher may request that arbitration be stayed pending resolution of said litigation.

If the acquisitions editor really wants the project, he or she should be able to arrange to have such a paragraph included in the contract. You may want to add a sentence stating that the arbitrator's fee will be paid by the loser.

If you believe your manuscript was declared unsatisfactory for reasons other than it really being so and there is no statement in your contract similar to the one in the preceding paragraph, you can attempt to negotiate to return the advance after you have received a contract for the book from another publisher. This is referred to as repayment through "first proceeds."

Proofs

The author agrees in this clause to check galley and page proofs and return them promptly. The author also agrees to pay (usually out of royalties) the typesetting costs for changes he or she makes that are not to correct printer's errors and that exceed a certain amount. This amount may be specified in dollars or as a percentage of the total cost of typesetting (e.g., 10 percent). If it is specified in dollars and the amount is relatively low, it may be possible to negotiate an increase. A few publishers charge for all changes that are made except those to correct printer errors.

Items Furnished by the Author

This clause specifies what the author is expected to furnish along with the manuscript (e.g., an index and instructor's manual). If the author does not furnish these, he or she probably will be charged for having them prepared.

Author's Warranty and Quoted Material (Indemnity Clause)

The author agrees both to protect the publisher from and defend the publisher in two types of litigation that could arise from publication of the work. One type is for copyright infringement. The author warrants that he or she is the sole owner of the copyright on the work and that there is no material in it that infringes on others' copyrights—that is, he or she warrants that permission was obtained for reproducing copyrighted material, except for that usable under the doctrine of "fair use."

The other type of litigation is for torts arising from comments made in the book (e.g., litigation for libel). The author agrees to pay the publisher's attorney fees and other litigation-related costs. One way an author can reduce the likelihood of such litigation is by having the manuscript examined (vetted) by an attorney for statements that could precipitate it.

Authors' groups hold that the indemnity clause places an unfair burden on their members. According to Irwin Karp, attorney for the Authors Guild (Memorandum to Book Publishers, March 9, 1978):

> Every publisher's standard contract contains an indemnity clause. It obliges the author to pay the publisher's expenses and attorneys fees incurred in claims or suits for libel and invasion of privacy; and judgments awarded against the publisher. Almost every publisher's standard indemnity clause requires the author to shoulder the publisher's expenses and attorneys fees *even though the book is not libelous or does not invade privacy.* . . . This unfair burden is . . . failure to obtain protection for authors under the insurance policies which shield publishing firms against liability [italics mine].

Editing

All book publishers copyedit manuscripts before having them typeset. If a manuscript is submitted on a computer disk, the editing may be done on it rather than on a printout. At a minimum copyediting involves identifying and correcting spelling and grammatical errors. It may also involve rewriting sentences and paragraphs. For example, sentences are likely to be rewritten that contain wordings that could be regarded as "sexist." Authors usually allow such alterations to be made if doing so does not change what they are trying to communicate.

Publishing Details

In the standard publishing contract, the author agrees to allow the publisher to make all decisions pertaining to the production and marketing of the book, including its title. While an acquisitions editor would be unlikely to change a book's title without the author's consent, he or she does have the right to do so if there is no language in the contract prohibiting it. Some authors have been successful in negotiating for changes that give them some control over title, production, and marketing. For example, they have had language added that requires the publisher to print the book in more than one color or on acid-free paper. The paper that most books are printed on, incidentally, is likely to deteriorate in fewer than 50 years. Although this usually isn't a cause of concern for textbook authors, it can be for those of scholarly monographs.

Some authors also have been successful in adding language that makes explicit the marketing plan for their book or material. Adding such language can be advantageous to the publisher as well as the author. One of the most frequent complaints that I have heard authors make about their publishers is that they did a less than adequate job marketing their books. If, however, an author knew and agreed to the marketing plan that the publisher planned to use for his or her book or material and it didn't sell well, the author probably would be less likely to blame the publisher than he or she otherwise would be.

Author's Copies

All authors receive some complimentary copies of their books. The number usually is between 5 and 12. They can purchase others at a discount. The number of copies the author will receive gratis and the discount at which he or she can purchase additional ones are specified in this clause. You may be able to have the number of gratis copies increased, particularly if you indicate that you need them for family and friends or if the acquisitions editor has refused most of your requests for contract changes. For the sake of "good will" he or she may want you to believe that your negotiation efforts yielded something. It costs the publisher very little to give them to you (often less than $3.00 a copy).

Revisions

The information in most textbooks and professional books will be out of date within a few years following publication. If a book has sold reasonably well and seems likely to continue doing so if brought up to date, the acquisitions editor probably will request a revision (i.e., a second edition). If the author either refuses to prepare one or agrees to do so but fails to deliver a satisfactory manuscript within a reasonable period of time, the publisher can contract with someone else to prepare it and deduct the cost from the author's future royalties. The name of the person who prepared the revision may appear on the cover and title page along with that of the original author. The publisher can also contract with someone after the author's death to prepare a revision if it still owns the copyright.

To protect yourself if you choose not to (or cannot) prepare a revision, you should negotiate to have the following restrictions added to this clause, if they are not already there (Levine, 1988):

1. Before the publisher can contract with someone to revise the book, you are to be given the opportunity to get someone to do it under your supervision.
2. The amount of money that can be paid to the person the publisher gets to revise the book will be limited to a maximum of 50 percent [or a lesser amount if you can negotiate it] of the royalties otherwise due you on that edition.
3. The contract the publisher enters into with the reviser should be on a "work for hire" basis so that he or she will have no rights to the work other than to receive the agreed-upon compensation for the edition being revised.
4. The manuscript for the revision should be submitted to you for approval and if you approve, your name will appear as an author.

There usually is a sentence in this clause that states that the terms of this agreement shall apply to each revision. You may or may not want to try to have it modified to read that the terms for each new edition will be negotiated. It depends on whether you believe you could command a higher royalty rate for subsequent editions because the book sold more copies than expected, average book royalty rates increased or some other reason. If you have it modified and your book doesn't sell as well as expected, you could end up having to accept a lower royalty rate for subsequent editions.

Subsidiary Rights

You authorize the publisher in this clause to act as your agent for the sale of publication rights to others. Payments received from such sales are split between you and the publisher—usually evenly. Subsidiary rights for educational and professional books and materials are most likely to be sold to professional book clubs, publishers of anthologies (including custom ones used as texts, referred to as coursepacks), foreign book publishers, and authors who are seeking permission to include material from your book in one of theirs.

This clause also specifies circumstances under which your royalty rate will be reduced. These may include mail-order sales made by the publisher or its subsidiaries and copies sold to persons in foreign countries. You should negotiate to have these rates increased, particularly if your book or material is likely to be sold mainly in this way. Although you are unlikely to be able to have the royalty percentage increased to that for other types of sales, you may be able to negotiate a better royalty percentage than that initially offered.

Finally, this clause specifies circumstances under which you will receive no royalty. These include ones in which copies are sold for less than manufacturing cost plus royalty. When a publisher believes that a book is unlikely to sell a significant number of additional copies, it may "remainder" the ones that *remain* in its warehouse. They are sold to a wholesaler for a fraction of their usual price. These are the books that bookstores and other retail outlets (e.g., K-Mart) sell at bargain prices. Authors do not receive a royalty from sales of such books. They also may not receive one for copies they purchase from the publisher at a discount.

Authors, of course, do not receive a royalty on examination copies of textbooks (and other books that can be used as texts) that publishers distributed gratis for adoption consideration. Some publishers send them only to instructors who request them. Others send them to all instructors who teach a course for which the book would be appropriate. The latter approach frequently results in a lot of gratis copies ending up in the used-book market (which reduces your royalty income). The official position of the Text and Academic Authors Association on this issue, incidentally, is that examination copies should only be sent to persons who request them. Some textbook publishers ask that examination copies be returned or paid for unless the book is adopted and a certain minimum number of copies (e.g., 10) are ordered.

Bookstores are permitted to return unsold copies. Consequently, if you were paid a royalty for copies that were returned, the amount will be subtracted from that which the publisher owes you. In some publishing contracts, particularly ones for textbooks, the publisher is allowed to withhold a certain percentage of the amount owed an author to minimize overpaying. If the amount seems excessive, you may want to negotiate to have it reduced.

Discontinuing Manufacture

This clause specifies what will occur when a book stops selling well. One statement that often is included in this clause specifies the minimum amount owed for which royalties will be paid on the next date when the contract indicates this is to be done. If the amount owed is less than the minimum specified in the contract (e.g., if it is less than $50), it will not be paid until the end of the next payment period at which it exceeds this amount. You may want to negotiate to have the statement deleted or the amount specified in it reduced (particularly if it is more than $50). Eventually sales of your book are likely to fall below this number, and you will certainly want to receive your royalty income when you are supposed to receive it.

Another statement that may appear in this clause allows the publisher to reduce your royalty percentage after a certain number of years (e.g., two) if the number of copies sold during a given year falls below a certain number. At some point sales are likely to be less than specified. Ask to have this statement deleted from the contract or the number designated in it reduced.

There also may be a statement in it that allows the publisher to withhold royalty income earned by future books from what is owed on this one. A publisher could, for example, subtract the money you received as an advance that exceeded the amount the book earned from royalty income earned by your next book. Even though you are not planning to write another book, ask to have the statement deleted. Point out that retaining it would penalize you for having more than one book published by the firm.

There should be a statement in this clause that specifies what will happen to the copyright when the publisher declares the book "out of print" and discontinues manufacture. If the statement does not indicate that the copyright will be returned to you at no cost, you should *insist* that it be replaced by one that does so.

Competing Works (Publications)

This clause appears in all publishing contracts. The author agrees not to publish a book or material with another firm that will compete with this one. You should negotiate to have what you are not allowed to publish described unambiguously—for example, you cannot publish a competing book for a specific course for first- and second-year students at a junior college. Also, if the clause states that a work is a competing one if it is so "in the opinion of the publisher," insist on these words being deleted. Otherwise, almost any book you write on the same general topic could be viewed by a court as a competing work.

Construction Treatment of Heirs

This clause specifies under which state's laws the contract will be interpreted. It also indicates that the publisher intends for the contract to be binding on an author's heirs. Furthermore, it declares that the contract is binding on anyone to whom the publisher sells or assigns rights transferred to it in the agreement (assuming that the publisher owns the copyright). This means, for example, that if the book is sold to (acquired by) another publisher, the royalty rate will be the same.

"Option" Clause

This clause gives the firm the right of "first refusal" for publishing the author's future books. Unless this clause is deleted, you will not be free to negotiate on future projects with another publisher. *Insist that it be deleted.* Almost all publishers are willing to do so if asked.

Other Clauses

The clauses discussed thus far are ones that publishers usually include in contracts. The following are some that they are unlikely to include but that you may want to negotiate to have included. Suggested wordings are from the model trade book contract distributed by the Authors Guild.

- The publisher shall publish the Work in the United States in English within 12 months after delivery of the manuscript of the completed Work. Should war, fire, or similar disaster beyond Publisher's control delay such publication, the book will be published within six months after termination of such disaster, but in no event later than 24 months after delivery of the said manuscript. If the Publisher fails to publish the Work within the applicable time period aforesaid, Author may terminate this Agreement on ten days written notice, and all rights thereupon shall revert to Author.

- Should Author be prevented by illness, accident, or military service from completing the manuscript, or changes, then the time of delivery of the manuscript, or changes, shall be extended until three months following the termination of the Author's incapacity or service, provided that if the manuscript, or changes, are not delivered within ___ months from the delivery date specified in this Agreement, or such later date that is mutually agreed to, Publisher may terminate the agreement on ten days written notice.

- All rights in the Work not specifically granted herein to Publisher are reserved to Author and may be exercised or disposed of by Author at any time during the term of this Agreement.

- Upon his or her written notice, Author or his or her designated representative may examine the books and records of Publisher which relate to sales of copies or licenses of the Work. If such examination discloses an error of more than 5% with respect to any royalty statement, Publisher shall reimburse Author or Author's costs of the examination; otherwise such costs shall be borne by Author.

- For the purposes of this Agreement the Work shall be deemed "in print" only when copies are available and offered for sale in the United States through normal channels. The Work shall not be deemed "in print" by virtue of the reproduction of copies by reprographic processes such as Xerox. If the Publisher fails to keep the Work in print, Author may at any time thereafter serve a written request on Publisher that the Work be placed "in print." Within 60 days of receipt of such request, Publisher should notify Author in writing whether it intends to comply with said request. If Publisher fails to give such notice or, having done so, fails to place the Work in print within six months after receipt of such request from Author, then, in either event, this Agreement shall automatically terminate and all rights granted to Publisher shall thereupon automatically revert to author.

- Publisher shall return the original manuscript of the Work to Author within 30 days after publication.

- If publisher is adjudicated [as] bankrupt or makes an assignment for the benefit of creditors or liquidates its business, this agreement shall thereupon terminate and all rights granted to Publisher shall automatically revert to Author.

For further information about negotiating book contracts, see Balkin (1985), Crawford (1977), Levine (1988), and Luey (1987).

PUBLISHING CONTRACTS FOR CO-AUTHORED PROJECTS

Our focus thus far has been on contracts for educational and professional books and materials that have a single author. Many such projects are co-authored by two or more persons. Co-authored projects fall into one of two general categories. The first is identical to the projects we have been discussing (i.e., those having a single author), except that the name of more than one author appears on the cover and title page. The second consists of edited volumes in which the names appearing on the cover and title page are those of the editors (who are likely to have authored a chapter or two themselves).

A publishing contract for a co-authored project that is not an edited volume is almost identical to that for one having a single author. The names of the co-authors appear on the first page of the contract and the contract is signed by all of them.

There are several issues with which a contract for a co-authored project has to deal that one having a single author does not. The contract should indicate how the royalties and the advance will be divided (i.e., the percentage each author will receive), whose name will come first on the title page, and whether the names are to be joined by "and," "with," or some other word. Furthermore, there should be a clause that specifies what will happen if a co-author fails to make his or her contribution to the project and the remaining one (or ones) want to complete it themselves or take on another co-author. It would be necessary to have the person's name removed from the contract. If the contract does not contain such a clause and a co-author loses interest in the project, it will be necessary to have the person agree to sign a release form that would be treated as a rider to the contract. The following is an example of such a form:

> This is to confirm our understanding that the Agreement dated [date on contract] between [names of authors] and [name of publisher] for the work entitled [title on contract] is hereby terminated and canceled in its entirety insofar as [name of author who is withdrawing] only is concerned and that there shall be no further liability or obligation as between [name of author who is withdrawing] and the remaining parties to the agreement, namely [remaining author(s) and publisher]. [Publisher] and [remaining author(s)] hereby ratify that the aforesaid agreement of [date on contract] for the work entitled [title on contract] remains in full force and effect as between [publisher] and [remaining author(s)].

The form would be dated and signed by all of the authors whose names appear on the contract. The author who is withdrawing could refuse to sign the form, thereby blocking publication of the project. Consequently, it is better to deal with this contingency proactively by including appropriate language in the contract with the publisher or in a joint collaboration agreement. Joint collaboration agreements are discussed elsewhere in this chapter.

The contract for a co-authored project that is an edited volume is also quite similar to that for one having a single author. The names that appear on the first page of the contract almost always are those of the editors. Authors of individual chapters may be asked to sign an agreement that would be treated as a rider to the contract. It would indicate both their responsibilities to the project and the compensation they will receive for meeting them. With regard to their responsibilities, it should state unambiguously that they are required to submit a manuscript to the editors that is "satisfactory to them in content, form, and style" by a certain date and that their failure to do so can result in their chapter(s) not being included in the book. Almost every person I know who has edited such a book has had at least one contributor fail to deliver a chapter that is of sufficiently high quality and/or fail to do so by the deadline specified in the publishing contract. While having contributors sign ("initial") such a statement is unlikely to prevent their becoming angry if their chapter is not included, it should reduce the likelihood that their anger will result in litigation.

Compensation for contributing a chapter to an edited book may be limited to receiving a complimentary copy of the book. This is the type of compensation that I have received most often for such a contribution. It could also include a percentage of the royalties, a flat fee, or some combination of the two. You are most likely to paid for your contribution to an edited volume if it is a textbook, particularly if it is one for a large-enrollment undergraduate course.

NEGOTIATING A JOINT COLLABORATION AGREEMENT

Our focus thus far has been on agreements (contracts) between publishers and authors. If you are co-authoring a book, you should also have a written agreement with your co-authors. A joint collaboration agreement should describe in detail the tasks assigned to each co-author, specify how royalty income will be divided, indicate deadlines by which chapters have to be drafted as well as what happens if deadlines are not met, specify who has the final word on questions of content and style, specify how authorship will be credited on the title page and specify how disputes will be resolved (e.g., by using an arbitrator from the American Arbitration Association if they cannot be resolved by the co-authors), specify conditions under which co-authors can and cannot use material from the joint work in other publications, and indicate what happens to a co-author's royalty income and authorship credit (on the title page and cover) when he or she dies or for some reason decides not to collaborate on future revisions of the book.

If your co-author (or co-authors) are friends, you may feel that there is no need to have a written agreement. Based on personal experience and the comments of several authors with whom I discussed this matter, I strongly recommend that you have one. Co-authoring a book can place a real strain on a friendship. As one author whom I interviewed commented: "If you're going to be co-authoring a book with a friend you have to consider whether the friendship is strong enough to make it through the process. The book can become such a big focus of your lives that you get into some real arguments, particularly if one of you is not meeting the other's expectations." Having such an agreement should prevent at least a few arguments. Consequently, having one is more likely to preserve than to destroy a friendship. Furthermore, because of the time spent negotiating the agreement, you and your co-author(s) are likely to be more aware of your responsibilities for the project than you would have been otherwise.

Prior to developing a joint collaboration agreement—indeed prior to deciding whether to co-author a book—you and your potential co-author(s) should have a frank discussion. In it, you should provide each other with answers to questions such as the following:

- What are my goals for writing this book?

- How do I take criticism? Do I take it well if it's constructive? Do I not take it well at first, but usually do after sleeping on it? Do I sometimes tend to be overly sensitive to criticism?

- How do I attack a writing project? Do I write a certain amount every day? Do I do it in a long burst just before a deadline? Do I work on it mostly during vacations or other periods when I have large blocks of time available?

- How do I relate to deadlines? Do I think a deadline is a deadline and should be met exactly? Do I think that deadlines should be flexible within reason? Do I frequently miss them?

- How often would I like to meet with my co-authors? Do I think we should meet on a regular basis (e.g., monthly) for progress reports and to toss ideas around or only when there is something that we need to do together?

- How long am I willing to devote myself to this project?
- What parts of doing a writing project are most odious to me?
- Where does this project stand in relation to my other priorities?

There is a representative joint collaboration agreement in Appendix B.

"SECOND THOUGHTS . . . "

I have assumed throughout this chapter that if you were offered an acceptable contract (based on your proposal and sample material), you would sign it and do the project. Occasionally an author has second thoughts about a project after being offered a contract because the niche for which it was intended has been filled. One of my interviewees reported turning down contracts for this reason:

> I was offered contracts on the basis of my proposal and I turned them down because I felt it was too risky. I knew from having talked with people how big the market was for human physiology books. I knew how many new ones had come out. I knew that there were two solid ones. It's simple arithmetic. I divided the marketplace by the number of books and the number wasn't very large.

There, of course, can be other reasons why an author may have second thoughts about doing a project for which a contract has been offered. He or she, for example, may no longer have adequate time available to do the project (possibly because of new family or professional responsibilities), or he or she may no longer be interested in doing it.

6

Doing the Project

After you have negotiated a publishing contract (assuming you are not planning to self-publish), your next task is to do the project. If your project is a book that is intended to be used as a text, you may also have to create an instructor's manual, student guide, and/or workbook and develop the specifications for other ancillaries, such as overhead transparencies, slides, videotapes, computerized testbanks, or instructional software. Software enhancements for textbooks are becoming more common, in part, because of the belief that students "learn better if textbook materials are enhanced with software that saves them the hassles of flipping pages and searching for items within text" (Brechner, 1992). You may also be expected to develop material for, or actually create, a site for your book on the World Wide Web.

After all of the text and graphic components of the project are completed, they are submitted to the acquisitions editor for review. The author probably will be asked to revise them, taking into consideration the editor's (and possibly several reviewers') suggestions. After a revision is submitted that is acceptable to the acquisitions editor, the project will be released for production (i.e., "launched").

Although this chapter focuses mainly on creating the text and graphics for a project, some information is provided about the production process. There are a number of production-related tasks for which an author is responsible, regardless of which company is publishing the project. Some guidelines are provided here for doing them.

CREATING THE TEXT AND GRAPHICS

The first step is to write the text and at least "rough out" the graphics. To do so, it is necessary to complete a number of tasks. There is more than one way in which most of them can be done. Options are presented here along with strategies that have proven useful to me and other authors.

Writing

Hardware Options for Writing

There are several decisions you have to make before beginning to write. One concerns what you will use for doing so. While almost all authors now use a microcomputer with word-processing software, some still use a typewriter. Before 1980 almost all books published in this century were written with a typewriter. I am mentioning this not because I advocate using a typewriter, but because I want you to be aware that you don't have to invest in a microcomputer if you don't already own one unless, of course, your contract calls for you to submit the manuscript "on disk" as well as "on paper." Actually, even if it called for you to submit the manuscript "on disk," you probably could still use a typewriter and scan the pages into a computer using optical character recognition (OCR) software. Although I now use a microcomputer, my first four books were written with a 1950s vintage manual typewriter.

There are several reasons why most authors have switched from typewriters to microcomputers. First, editing does not require retyping pages. Sentences and paragraphs can be added, deleted, modified, and relocated without having to do so. Second, editing can be facilitated by using software that checks spelling and grammatical usage and suggests synonyms. Third, manuscripts for new editions are easier to prepare because material that is being retained does not have to be retyped. Finally, it is possible to copyedit and typeset from word-processor files. Authors who self-publish, incidentally, usually typeset in this way.

Even though it is more efficient to write a manuscript with a computer than with a typewriter, doing so has the potential to adversely affect the quality of the writing. This is particularly likely to happen if you do all your editing on a monitor screen—rather than on both a monitor screen and a printout. Your writing may suffer because you will be unable to view more than 20 lines at a time (unless, of course, you have a full-page monitor). The simple solution is to make printouts of chapter drafts and use them for editing.

Most authors now use either a Macintosh or IBM-compatible microcomputer, but any computer can be used for which there is word-processing software. Early drafts of this book and others I wrote before the early 1990s were prepared with an Apple IIC microcomputer and AppleWorks software. When I switched from an Apple II to a Macintosh, I used file conversion software to "translate" the Apple II word-processor files for my books into ones that could be read and modified by the Macintosh version of Microsoft Word. If I had switched to an IBM-compatible computer (rather than to a Macintosh), the conversion could have been accomplished just as easily.

Some authors still do first drafts of chapters on legal pads. In one survey of college textbook authors during the early 1990s, 27 percent acknowledged doing so. Several of the authors whom I interviewed commented that drafting chapters in this way improved the quality of their writing because they found themselves considering alternatives to every word, phrase, sentence, and paragraph while they were keyboarding what they wrote. Furthermore, they indicated that drafting chapters in this way enabled them to work on their manuscript anywhere and for as long as they wanted. They were not restricted, for example, by the amount of power remaining in the battery of a laptop computer.

Much of the material that I wrote during the past 25 years was initially drafted on sheets of paper. The sheets of paper were sometimes in pads or three-ring binders but other times they were carried folded in a shirt pocket. I always edited the material while keyboarding it in the ways that my interviewees reported doing so. And drafting material in this manner enabled me to work on a project wherever I was while traveling.

There are, of course, other ways to draft manuscripts. One of the authors whom I interviewed indicated that his way of doing it utilizes a tape recorder, a legal pad, and a computer:

> The way I write is I think a great deal about what I'm going to write. And I'll be concentrating on a given subject area which will constitute a chapter eventually. And I keep thinking about that. And then I work up the illustrations—charts and graphs—and ex-

amples. Then, having done that preliminary work on the subject, I will dictate into a tape recorder the whole chapter at once around all of those examples and illustrations. I have a chapter. So, I play it back to myself and I write it down in longhand in pencil and I revise it as I write. Then I type the whole thing and I revise as I'm doing this. This is a real rough draft. Next, I retype it again in more finished copy. That's what the publisher gets. I have rewritten and retyped three times. That's exactly the way I write. I've done it all my life.

There is no one right way to write!

For further information about hardware options for writing, see Schultz (1990).

Where to Write

Another decision you will have to make is where to write. Some authors do it at their office, some at home, and some at both. I do it at both. If you are using a computer and are planning to write at both your home and office, you will either have to have a computer at home that is compatible with the one at your office or a portable (laptop) one.

Some authors, including myself, occasionally write at other locations, including hotel rooms and lobbies, airports, and restaurants. I am an "early morning person," and when I travel, I usually write at a restaurant for several hours while having breakfast.

It is advantageous to be able to work on a manuscript wherever you are. Rather than having to rely solely on large blocks of time to draft it, you will be able to take advantage of some of the small ones that occur almost every day. Their duration may be 30 minutes or fewer. They can occur at work—between classes and/or meetings. They can arise at home when you wake up early or when you are tempted to watch television programs you really have no interest in watching. And they can come about while you are traveling. Even if they last for only a few minutes, you may be able to make significant progress on a project by utilizing them. "William Carlos Williams, the physician-poet, . . . turned out a large body of work during office hours by writing *single lines of poetry between patients*. Williams kept pad and pencil in his desk drawer and between the time one patient left his office and the next entered, he would scribble a line—and sometimes two or more! (*Principles of Good Writing*, 1969, p. 90).

When such blocks of time occur when you don't have a computer available, you can write on a pad (or whatever paper is available) and keyboard the material later. The topic about which you write does not have to be the one with which you are currently dealing. All word-processing programs enable you to write paragraphs in any order and later arrange them appropriately.

Few authors can be productive if they are constantly being inter-rupted. Creating an interruption-free environment in your home can be particularly difficult if you have young children. One of my inter-viewees attempted to do it in a rather novel way:

> When my daughter was in fifth grade I did much of my writing at home and she would sometimes come in and interrupt me. Once to discourage her from doing it I said "Becky, every time you come in here and interrupt me it costs me ten cents a word." Well, she came in after that and said, "I've got a great idea, Dad. Put the end at the end of every chapter and then you can make another twenty cents."

Establishing a Daily Writing Schedule

As I have indicated previously, one of the secrets to finding enough time to complete a project is utilizing the small "chunks" that occur in most people's schedules almost every day. Another is establishing a schedule that will enable you to work on the project at about the same time almost every day, for at least 30 minutes. This strategy is used by many authors (including myself). Even if your schedule only enables you to work on a project for 30 minutes a day, you can make significant progress.

> The importance of a regular schedule—this same half hour every day—is vital; a definite rhythm is created both mentally and physi-cally, and the writer automatically goes to his [or her] desk at that certain time, drawn by habit. The brain too . . . quickly learns to op-erate efficiently at such times. . . . Once the pattern of a daily half hour at a stated time is set, nothing short of disaster will keep you from writing. . . . The mere fact that such a routine is habit-forming . . . will condition you to greater output. (*Principles of Good Writ-ing*, 1969, pp. 88, 91)

I have used this strategy for the past 25 years. I write every morning (immediately after waking and having a cup or two of coffee) for 30 minutes to an hour. I have been able to draft manuscripts for 300- to 350-page books in approximately 18 months by doing so.

One reservation that you are likely to have about this strategy is that you need time to think before you write and, consequently, much (perhaps most) of each 30-minute period would likely be spent thinking. While only a half-hour may be scheduled for writing, the preparation for doing it is likely to take place all day. Somerset Maugham, the novelist, commented in an interview:

> The author does not only write while he's at his desk, he writes all day long, when he is thinking, when he is reading, when he is experiencing, everything he sees and feels is significant to his purpose and, consciously or unconsciously, he is forever storing and making over his impressions. (Quoted in *Principles of Good Writing*, 1969)

Several authors whom I interviewed made similar comments.

> I write almost every night. And I think about it during the day and get thoughts organized in my mind so that when I come home I can sit down and actually do it. I have done a whole chapter in one sitting because I had it all in my head.

> The book constantly is on my mind. How do I want to conceptualize this? Can I say it this way? In thinking about it, I found I was preoccupied by it almost 24 hours a day.

Outlining

It is necessary to prepare a detailed chapter outline before beginning to write. The one that you included in your proposal may or may not have sufficient detail. Chapter outlines are one of the principal tools used by book authors. Few write without them. Good outlines help authors to develop their thoughts logically. They also help them ensure that all relevant topics will be dealt with and that the presentation will not be repetitive. Furthermore, they help to make the book easier to read (because the writing has greater unity) and to keep the writing moving forward (by naming the topic that is to be written about next).

Most authors revise their chapter outlines while they are writing. New topics and better orderings of topics often occur to them while they are doing so. Consequently, the content of a chapter outline should be regarded as tentative and subject to change throughout the period that a manuscript is being drafted and edited.

Software for outlining is available for all computers. Most word-processing packages (such as WordPerfect or Microsoft Word) contain such software. Also, there are independent outlining programs available and their files can be read by a word-processing program. Most such software allows paragraphs, drawings, and tables to be included in an outline. Some also allow photographs, sound recordings, and videotape segments to be included in one. Consequently, an outline can serve as a database for storing material that is to be included in a book. Text, tables, drawings, and photographs can be scanned into such a database.

Two basic approaches can be used for defining chapters and assigning topics to them. One is to proceed from *chapters to topics* and the other from *topics to chapters*. The first ordinarily is used when books on the subject already exist, either in your field or related ones. You use their tables of contents as a starting point for yours and their indexes as a starting point for both identifying topics to discuss and assigning them to chapters.

The second of these approaches—proceeding from topics to chapters—usually is used when a book is the first one dealing with a subject. You identify the topics you want to discuss and assign them to categories. From these categories you define chapters. A given category could be a portion of a chapter or an entire one. It is important when using this approach to be certain that there are no "orphan" topics. Their presence indicates that additional chapters are needed or that at least one existing chapter has to be redefined.

Drafting the Manuscript

Once you have developed a reasonably complete *first approximation* of your outline, you should begin to write. The outline for each chapter should be transferred to the word-processor file for it (assuming that you are using a computer to draft the manuscript). It is advisable to have a separate file for each chapter, unless the entire manuscript will be less than 150 pages long.

Sentences and paragraphs can be "cut" from the outline and "pasted" in the manuscript. This makes it unnecessary to rekeyboard them. Illustrations and tables that were stored in the outline can be incorporated into the manuscript in this same way.

If this is your first book, you are likely to be overwhelmed by the prospect of drafting a book-length manuscript. A strategy that some authors use to cope with this feeling is to focus on the specific task they have to do next—for example, writing a certain number of words—rather than on the end product (a completed manuscript). Most experienced book authors set a daily or weekly rate for themselves—one they can easily achieve and frequently exceed (*Principles of Good Writing*, 1969). One of the authors whom I interviewed commented as follows on his weekly rate: "I like the idea of word quotas as a writer. A book looks like such an unattainable end product. You ask yourself, how the heck am I ever going to write 150,000 words? I try to write 3,000 words a week—500 words a day and I give myself a day off."

Another reason why the prospect of drafting a book-length manuscript may seem overwhelming is feeling that you have to make each sentence "perfect" before moving on. This attitude can impede the drafting process by making working on the manuscript adversive. If you are having difficulty editing what you have written and feel that you have to do so before proceeding, you probably will not be looking forward to your next writing session. Consequently, you may procrastinate on beginning it.

The attitude toward writing that is most likely to facilitate progress is viewing it as a two-stage process. The first is getting down what you want to communicate and the second is revising (editing) what you have written so that your "message" will be clear to the reader. The following remarks by Roger H. Garrison (from *Principles of Good Writing*, 1969) indicate the importance of the latter:

> Nearly all first drafts, even those of skilled writers, are verbose, awkward, and disconnected. Ideas have gaps in one place and overflow in another. Sentences and paragraphs are turgid and muddy. A first draft is like the slow emerging of a statue from a block of stone. The rough shape of the work may be plain, but there is much chisel work and smoothing to be done.

During the first stage, you shouldn't be too concerned about word choice, spelling, grammatical usage, or sentence structure. If ideas occur to you for improving these, it's acceptable to do a little editing, so long as doing it doesn't interfere with getting down your thoughts. Most experienced authors do very little editing before they finish drafting a manuscript. However, if knowing there are lots of errors disturbs you and keeps you from moving forward, then do what editing you think is necessary.

During this first stage, you shouldn't be too concerned about checking information for accuracy. Doing so can interfere with your getting down your thoughts. It is important, however, to have a strategy for identifying the information that you want to check later for accuracy. The writer, James Michener, used and recommended the following strategy:

> Because in this first draft I am struggling to outline a narrative pro-
> gression, I do not interrupt my thought processes to check with al-
> manacs, atlases, or encyclopedias to verify dates, spellings, or other
> data; I am aware as I type that I don't have the facts, but I am secure
> in the knowledge that I'll be able to find them when I go back to
> edit. So, for uncertainties I . . . type in what I guess to be the correct
> information adding immediately after the data a series of question
> marks: "Magna Carta was granted by King John???? in 1215????,"
> with the intention of dealing with them later when I have my re-
> search books at hand. I advocate this strategy because the forward
> motion of the narrative is all important. (Michener, 1992, p. 7)

You can use your word processor's "find" command to quickly locate
the information you have to check for accuracy by asking it to find all instances of "????."

Revising (Editing) the Manuscript

The most important part of the manuscript-drafting process is the
first—communicating your unique knowledge. Your book or material
will be judged primarily on the usefulness of its content to consumers.
Although you certainly should strive to make the writing as clear and interesting as you can and the spelling and grammatical usage as correct as
you can, the copyeditor can be expected to fill the gap if your efforts fall
a little short in this regard. (The role of the copyeditor is discussed elsewhere in this chapter.)

If there are serious problems with your writing that you are unable to
correct, it may be possible to contract with someone to rewrite the
manuscript, possibly a colleague or a professional freelance writer. The
contract with such a person should state that for services rendered he or
she will be paid an hourly fee, given a percentage of the royalty income,
and/or be designated a co-author. You may be able to get some help in
locating a freelance writer from the Authors Guild or the Text and Academic Authors Association.

An acquisitions editor may anticipate the need for a freelance writer
before a manuscript is written. He or she may, for example, be uncertain
about an author's ability to write at the level needed to communicate to
college freshmen. Consequently, a clause similar to the following (from
a contract of mine for an introductory text) may be added to the contract to ensure that the book will be written at an appropriate level:

> An additional 1½% reserved for a freelance writer/copy editor will be paid to the Author on the first 10,000 copies sold in the first edition in the event that the manuscript does not require rewriting to render it appropriate in style and level for undergraduate students. All work provided by the freelance writer/copy editor will be submitted to the Author to insure that its content and meaning have not been materially altered.

Incidentally, if you are writing a textbook for an introductory course, it can be disastrous to write it to impress instructors with the depth of your knowledge if doing so causes it to be written at too high a level to appeal to students. Negative feedback from them can discourage instructors from continuing to adopt it.

Your primary focus while editing the manuscript should be on eliminating grammatical and spelling errors and on communicating clearly to your intended audience. The book by King (1991), although intended for physicians, presents suggestions that should help any textbook or professional book author to communicate more clearly. And the book by Strunk and White (1979) can help you to identify and eliminate common grammatical errors. Other books on writing that you may find helpful are those by Van Til (1986) and Zinsser (1988).

You should present your material as interestingly as you can. The amount of attention that people will pay to what you write will be determined, in part, by how interesting it is to them. While subject matter certainly influences a reader's level of interest in a topic, the manner in which the topic is communicated is also important. The particular topics with which a book deals will, of course, influence how easily this can be done. It would be easier, for example, to make an introductory psychology book interesting to the average reader than an introductory statistics one.

Several strategies can be used to make a book more interesting to readers who don't have a high level of interest in the topics dealt with in it. One is to include as many examples as possible that both clarify concepts and are relevant to the readers' interests. For example, in a clinical research design text intended for students majoring in speech pathology, at least some of the examples that are used to illustrate single-subject research designs should be ones that are relevant to documenting therapy outcome.

Another strategy that you can use to make a book more interesting than it would otherwise be is to write in an "oral" style—one closer to that in a transcribed lecture than that in a typical journal article. There are several ways to achieve this writing style. One is to dictate first drafts of chapters, using an audiocassette tape recorder or a dictating machine. Incidentally, if some of the topics about which you will be writing are ones about which you lecture, you may want to tape-record lectures in which you discuss them.

A second way to achieve an oral writing style is to read aloud what you have written. Visualize the audience to whom you are trying to communicate (for a textbook it would consist of students). If a sentence probably would sound awkward to a lecture audience, change the wording.

You may be able to increase interest in your book by making it more visually appealing. You might include attractive photographs, line drawings, and/or other types of figures. Or insert sidebars—that is, interesting part-page or whole-page excerpts from other publications that pertain to topics you are discussing. Perhaps include exercises or assignments that readers are likely to look upon as both worthwhile and challenging (e.g., simulations). If a computer is needed to do them, the software can be furnished with the book, given to instructors who adopt it, or placed on a site on the World Wide Web. With the level of interest most students now have in "surfing" the Internet, a Web site for a book is highly likely to generate interest in the book if the site is well designed. The Web site can augment the usefulness of a book in several ways: providing computational and other exercises for students (responses to which can be automatically e-mailed to the instructor), links to other sites on the Web where there is information that can increase a student's depth of understanding of certain concepts and principles presented in the book, and frequently updated supplementary readings. It can even contain a bulletin board that will enable students to communicate with the book's author(s).

Another issue to which you have to be sensitive when editing your manuscript is "sexism." Most publishers insist that the books and materials they publish be as free of sexist language as possible. An example of such language is using the masculine pronoun (he or him) to refer to professionals in a particular field. As the McGraw-Hill Book Company has pointed out in its booklet "Guidelines for Bias-Free Publishing" (n.d., pp. 11–12),

> The English language lacks a nongender-specific singular personal pronoun. Although masculine pronouns have generally been used for reference to a hypothetical person or to humanity in general (in

such constructions as "anyone . . . he" and "each child opened his book"), the following alternatives are recommended as preferable.

- Recast to eliminate unnecessary gender-specific pronouns.

NO	YES
When a mechanic is checking the brakes, he must observe several precautions.	When checking the brakes, a mechanic must observe several precautions.

- Use a plural form of the pronoun—a very simple solution and often the best.

When mechanics check the brakes, they must observe several precautions.

- Recast in the passive voice, making sure there is no ambiguity.

When a mechanic is checking the brakes, several precautions must be observed.

- Use *one* or *we.*

When checking the brakes, we must observe several precautions.

- Use a relative clause.

A mechanic who is checking the brakes must observe several precautions.

- Recast to substitute the antecedent for the pronoun.

NO	YES
The committee must consider both the character of the applicant and his financial responsibilities.	The committee must consider both the character and financial responsibilities of the applicant.

- Use *he or she, him or her, or his or her.* (These constructions have passed easily into wide use.)

The committee must consider the character of the applicant and his or her financial responsibilities.

- Alternate male and female expressions and examples.

NO	YES
I've often heard supervisors say, "He's not the right man for the job," or "She lacks the qualifications for success."	I've often heard supervisors say, "She's not the right person for the job," or "He lacks the qualifications for success."

There also are other suggestions in this booklet for eliminating sexism. For further help in doing so, see *Fields' Reference Book for Non-sexist Words and Phrases* (1987) and Miller and Swift (1988).

A related issue to be aware of while editing your manuscript—particularly if it is a textbook—is "insensitivity to cultural differences." It is important that we do not inadvertently bias what we write with our own culture-related values and beliefs. Furthermore, because textbooks transmit values as well as information, you may be able through your writing (particularly through your choice of examples) to promote increased sensitivity to and acceptance of cultural diversity.

The Front Matter

After you have drafted and edited the manuscript, all that remains to be written (besides the index) is the front matter. The front matter consists of the title page, dedication, table of contents, list of figures, preface, and acknowledgments (which may be incorporated into the preface). The preface is quite important because some book reviewers base their description of a book largely on information in it. Your publisher will provide guidelines for structuring the front matter portion of the manuscript.

Permission to Use Copyrighted Material

Most educational and professional books include material (text and/or illustrations) from books and journals that are copyrighted. It almost always is necessary to secure the written permission of the copyright owner to reproduce illustrations. This is not the case for text. The reason is the doctrine of "fair use"—a component of the Copyright Act of 1976 (our current copyright law). This doctrine "allows copying without permission from, or payment to, the copyright owner when the use is *reasonable and not harmful* to the rights of the copyright owner" [italics mine] (Dible, 1978, p. 142). Section 107 of the act (part of which is reproduced below), which deals with fair use, seems somewhat vague, but it does provide some general guidelines for deciding when this doctrine is applicable.

> In determining whether the use made of a work in any particular case is a fair use, the factors to be considered shall include—
>
> 1. the purpose and character of the use, including whether such use is of a commercial nature or is for nonprofit educational purposes;
> 2. the nature of the copyrighted work;
> 3. the amount and substantiality of the portion used in relation to the copyrighted work as a whole; and

4. the effect of the use on the potential market for or value of the copyrighted work.

With regard to the first of these guidelines, the courts tend to look upon professional books and textbooks (with the possible exception of highly profitable ones for introductory courses) as being closer to the nonprofit educational end of the commercial continuum than to the trade book end of it. Consequently, they tend to define fair use for them fairly liberally.

With regard to the second, the courts tend to define fair use fairly conservatively for copyrighted works that are not professional or academic books or journals. Consequently, it is probably a good idea to get written permission before quoting even a few lines of text from a publication that is not a professional or academic one.

The third of these is one of the two most important determiners of whether a court is likely to look upon this doctrine as being applicable. Quoting more than a line or two from a very short work (e.g., a poem) definitely requires written permission. While there isn't general agreement among specialists on copyright law on the amount it is safe to quote from an article in a professional journal or from a professional or academic book without written permission, most would agree that up to *250 words* is permissible.

The final guideline—the impact that the use is likely to have on sales of the work—is the other important determiner of the applicability of this doctrine. The situation in which it can be applied with most confidence is one in which it would be far-fetched for a copyright owner to claim that the use adversely affected sales or would be likely to do so. A court would almost always regard it as being far-fetched for the publisher of a professional or scientific journal to claim that quoting fewer than 200 words from an article reduced sales of the journal. On the other hand, if chapters of a book were copied without permission for classroom use, the situation would be entirely different. A court would be unlikely to regard it as being far-fetched that the copying of chapters for this purpose resulted in a loss of sales for the book from which the chapters were copied.

Most publishers provide forms for requesting permission to reproduce copyrighted material. Rather than using the forms I am given, I generate one with database software (Appendix C) that is quite similar to my publisher's. In addition to reducing the amount of information that has to be filled in for each request, using it has another advantage.

On the form provided by my publisher, there is a space for the copyright owner to indicate the fee he or she will charge for granting permission. Its presence is likely to cause at least a few copyright owners to charge a fee who would not otherwise do so. This is of concern to me because I am responsible for paying permission fees. Those copyright owners who do charge a fee attach a form to mine indicating the amount.

For further information about fair use and copyright, see Blue (1990), Bunnin and Beren (1988), Kozak (1990a), Luey (1987), Novick and Chasen (1984), and Strong (1984).

Illustrations

Unless your project is a textbook for a large-enrollment undergraduate course, your contract it likely to require you to both provide and pay for illustrations (drawings and photographs). There are a number of suggestions in this section that may enable you to reduce the amount that you will have to pay for providing them.

You may be able to acquire some of the photographs and drawings that you need from professional books, journal articles, advertisements, and product catalogs. Some professional and scientific journals will allow you to use photographs and drawings from papers in them without paying a fee if the authors of the papers in which they appear are agreeable. Also, some academic and professional book publishers—particularly university presses—will allow you to use illustrations from books they have published either without cost or for a nominal fee. Furthermore, copies of photographs and drawings from advertisements and product catalogs often can be acquired and used without cost if their source is acknowledged.

Almost all of the illustrations in books and other printed materials are now created from drawings and photographs that are scanned into a computer and manipulated ("retouched"). The drawings and photographs scanned may be originals or from journals, books, or other publications. If they are from publications, they may be scanned directly from the pages on which they appear or from high quality photocopies of them. Drawings that are scanned from publications usually reproduce closer in quality to the original than do photographs.

Once a drawing or photograph is scanned into a computer, it can be manipulated ("retouched") in a number of ways. For example, its size can be increased or decreased. If it is in color, it can be converted to black and white. Its contrast can be increased or decreased. If it is a drawing, portions of it can be "erased" and new elements (e.g., labels) added. If it is a photograph, part of the image (e.g., a distracting background) can be eliminated and/or a part of another photograph (e.g., one with a more appropriate background) can be added to it. This, incidentally, is how the half human–half animal and other bizarre photographs that appear in supermarket tabloids are created. The sophisticated image-manipulation software that is currently available enables almost any modification to be made to a drawing or photograph. Many of these modifications can be made by someone who has little or no artistic ability.

Drawings

There are two options for creating graphs and other drawings you are unable to acquire. You can have them created by a freelance illustrator from rough sketches or you can generate them yourself using a computer. Even though the first of these options may (but not necessarily will) yield drawings that are more attractive than the second, it is unlikely to yield ones that are more accurate. In fact, a drawing that you create is more likely to communicate what you want to communicate because you know specifically what it should be and an illustrator may not. Another advantage of doing it yourself is that it's a lot cheaper.

Software is available for converting sets of numbers into graphs that are suitable for publication. Almost any type of graph can be drawn in this way. You supply the data and a description of the type of graph you want and the computer does the rest. You can use either a program intended specifically for this purpose (e.g., DeltaGraph Professional) or a spreadsheet one that has this capability (e.g., Microsoft Excel). You can submit graphs drawn in this way as files on a computer disk, as laser or inkjet printouts, or both. Most publishers prefer to have graphs and other drawings submitted on disk because they don't have to scan them. If you hire an illustrator to draw graphs, he or she will probably draw them with this type of software. Consequently, they will be no more attractive (but possibly less accurate) than ones you draw yourself.

There is software available for making drawings other than graphs. There are several types of drawings that almost anyone can produce with such software after a few hours of practice. One is charts (e.g., flow and organizational ones). All that producing a chart usually entails is drawing some geometric shapes (e.g., rectangles), arranging them appropriately on a page, connecting them by lines or arrows, and placing text in (or adjacent to) them to indicate what they represent. With a drawing program, such as MacDraw Professional, every element (geometric shape, connecting line, word) is a separate "object" that can be moved or modified without affecting other parts of the drawing. Consequently, mistakes can be corrected easily. Charts, like graphs, can be submitted on disk, printed on paper, or both.

Another type of drawing that requires little or no artistic ability to produce is one that is a slightly modified version of an existing drawing, particularly one that only requires you to remove ("erase") elements and/or change text. The existing drawing is scanned into the computer and modified with a drawing program (see Beale and Cavuoto, 1989, for an in-depth discussion of how this is done).

If the resulting drawing is quite similar to the original and you do not own the copyright on the original, you should probably request permission to reproduce the modified drawing from the copyright owner. I include the word "probably" because if the drawing is "generic," permission to reproduce may not be necessary. Unfortunately, there are no generally accepted guidelines for what constitutes a "generic" drawing. Consequently, even though it may not be necessary to obtain permission to reproduce a drawing that most people would classify as "generic," it probably would be a good idea to do so.

You probably will have to rely on a freelance illustrator for complex drawings, such as anatomical ones. Producing them can be quite expensive. If you know before you negotiate a contract that you are going to need some, you should try to get the publisher to agree to pay part of the expense. Also, you should consider using existing drawings. Even if the fee that you would have to pay to reproduce them is not nominal, the amount is likely to be less than what you would have to pay to have them drawn.

Photographs

There are several ways that you can get the photographs you need that are not available for free or a nominal charge from one of the sources previously mentioned. These are taking the photographs yourself, having them taken by a professional photographer, or purchasing them from an agency that sells stock photographs.

If you have access to a camera—such as a 35-mm single-lens reflex—you may be able to take at least a few of the photographs you need. You may also be able to abstract them from videotapes that were made with a camcorder. The quality of the image will be somewhat better than the one you see on a television screen when you pause the tape.

If you need photographs of a general nature (e.g., candid photographs of children) and are unable to take them yourself, it may be cheaper to purchase them from an agency that sells stock photos than to have them taken by a professional photographer. The larger ones have hundreds of thousands of photographs in their files. Some of these agencies are listed in the book *Photographer's Market*, which is published by Writer's Digest.

Two other sources for photographs of a general nature (from 1860 to the present) are the Library of Congress and the National Archives. Both charge very little for them. An 8" × 10" black-and-white print from the National Archives cost less than $10.00 when this chapter was written.

If there are people in some of your photographs who can be recognized, you should have them sign a model release form. There is a general-purpose one in Appendix C.

Ancillaries

Your publisher will provide detailed instructions for preparing ancillary materials. You are most likely to have to prepare them if your book is a text for an introductory course.

SUBMITTING THE MANUSCRIPT AND RELATED MATERIALS

Your final responsibility for the preproduction phase of the project is delivering the manuscript, illustrations, ancillaries, and permission forms to your acquisitions editor. Many publishing contracts call for you to deliver two copies of the manuscript. This clause dates from pre-copier days—when manuscripts were typed and copies were carbon copies. Although all my contracts have called for me to do this, I have never sent more than one copy nor have I ever been asked to do so. You, of course, should make a copy for yourself. In fact, you should make a copy of everything you send to the publisher, including permission forms.

The acquisitions editor, after receiving the manuscript, will decide whether it is "satisfactory in style, form, and content" and if it isn't, what changes have to be made to make it satisfactory. Some utilize input from reviewers for making this decision. It usually takes several months for reviews to be commissioned and completed. If the manuscript is reviewed, you will receive copies of the reviews as well as suggestions for revisions from your acquisitions editor. Otherwise, you will just receive the latter. After you have revised the manuscript to the acquisition editor's satisfaction (assuming, of course, that he or she considered the manuscript to be salvageable), the book will be "launched"—that is, released for production.

THE PRODUCTION PROCESS

The production process usually is initiated by a launch meeting. Participants ordinarily include the acquisitions editor, the production editor, the book-manufacturing buyer, the marketing manager, the art director, and the designer. A detailed schedule is prepared that projects dates for every aspect of the production process from the start of copyediting to the delivery of books to the warehouse. Figure 6.1 provides an overview of your responsibilities during this process.

Prior to or immediately following the launch meeting, the production editor probably will give a copy of the manuscript to the person who will be copyediting the book, the person(s) who will be obtaining cost estimates and making design decisions about the book (including arranging for sample pages), and the person(s) who will be developing and/or implementing a marketing plan for the book. The production editor is the person who arranges to have done what has to be done to transform a manuscript (plus probably at least a few illustrations) into a book. He or she will be the main person with whom you will interact during the production process.

There are several production-related tasks that usually are initiated while a manuscript is being copyedited. They include making decisions about page and typographical design and arranging for the following: artwork (including that for the cover), typesetting, printing, and binding. Most, if not all, of these tasks probably will be done by freelancers (i.e., independent contractors) rather than by employees of the publisher. Even a production editor can be a freelancer! In fact, a freelancer (fortunately, the same one) served as the production editor for my last five books.

One of the first production tasks is doing a *cast-off*, which is an estimate of the length of the book. A cast-off has two functions. The first is to furnish an approximate page count when requesting estimates from printers and binders. And the second is to make design decision adjustments—including ones for sizes of type and illustrations—that will put

Figure 6.1
Author's Responsibilities during the Production Process

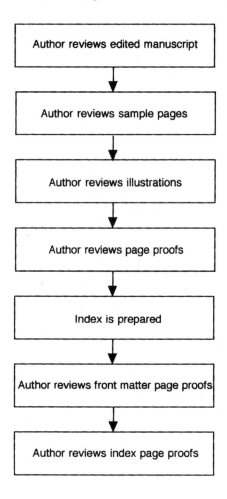

the page count at a particular number. This is necessary both to keep the book within budget and to utilize the last signature fully (or nearly so). Books are printed on large sheets of paper called signatures. Most book signatures contain 8, 16, or 32 book pages. An 8-page signature has four pages on each side.

After a firm has been selected to typeset your book, the production editor will request sample pages. These will be ones that illustrate various aspects of the book's page layout and typography. You may be asked to comment on and/or approve them.

The marketing manager (or a member of his or her staff) will begin to develop a plan for marketing your book while the manuscript is being copyedited. Much of the information used for developing it will be taken from the marketing questionnaire you are required to complete. The information that is likely to be requested includes the following: the principal features of your book, the audience for which it is intended, how it differs from and can be claimed to be superior to competing texts, periodicals to which copies should be sent for review, suggestions for where it should be advertised and otherwise promoted, and the groups (organizations) who are likely to be interested in the book. The plan developed for marketing it could include any or all of the following: listing it in *Books in Print*, mailing copies to journals for review, sending sets of page proofs to professional book clubs, sending examination copies to teachers, selling rights (including translation ones) to foreign publishers, making working professionals aware of what it could do for them by mailing them a brochure or catalog in which this is described, advertising it in professional journals, advertising it at a site on the World Wide Web (e.g., the publisher's "home page"), and displaying it at professional meetings. The marketing of educational and professional books and materials is dealt with further in Chapter 7.

The interval between a book's "launch" meeting and its being available for sale is usually between six months and two years. For most books, its duration is about a year. Authors have a number of responsibilities while their book is in production. These responsibilities are summarized in Figure 6.1 and described below.

Checking the Copyediting

The copyeditor marks the manuscript for typesetting. The copyeditor also checks the manuscript for accuracy, particularly the references. He or she makes certain that all papers and books cited are included in the reference list and that author's names are spelled the same in both. In addition, he or she checks the manuscript for errors in typing, spelling, punctuation, and grammar, and attempts to improve the clarity of sentences that are vague or confusing.

Your publisher will ask you to carefully read the copyedited manuscript before the book is typeset. You will be expected to review all the changes the copyeditor made, particularly those involving the rewording of sentences. It is easy for a copyeditor to inadvertently change the meaning of a sentence when trying to make it clearer. Even the most expert copyeditor is likely to do this at least a few times in a book-length manuscript. Although you shouldn't accept the copyeditor's suggestions for rewording sentences when doing so would change their meaning, you should try rewording them yourself to make them clearer. If a copyeditor does not understand what you are trying to communicate, a reader may not either. You also are expected to respond to queries (questions) from the copyeditor. These usually are written on small pieces of paper (referred to as tags) that are glued to the edge of the manuscript page in the proximity of the sentence, or sentences, to which they refer. Finally, you will be asked to reread the entire manuscript for content and make any changes you feel are necessary. This will be your last opportunity to do so with the publisher's blessing. Resetting type is expensive. You will be charged for changes you make in galley proofs and page proofs that are not to correct printer errors and exceed an amount specified in your contract (see Chapter 5).

There is another reason why it is undesirable to make changes in page proofs. Page proofs are used for indexing. If you add more than a few words to a page or delete more than a few words from one, the rearrangement of material could result in some page numbers in the index being incorrect. Consequently, your best strategy if you have to add material to a page is to delete approximately the same amount of material (number of characters) from it. And if you have to delete material from a page, add approximately the same amount of material to it.

There are a number of things you can do when formatting a manuscript for printing and editing that can facilitate the copyediting process. Among them are the following (Rodberg, 1992, p. 13):

- Double space EVERYTHING: text, tables, and most especially references. *Reason*: Many marks pertaining to typography will have to be inserted. Reference style is especially subject to changes and transpositions. The copy editor needs room.

- Leave wide margins: ideally 1.5 inches all round. *Reason*: Copyeditors and production editors need margins for table and figure callouts, typecoding, and those all-important queries to you. Although most typesetters can read inscriptions small enough for the head of a pin, they'd rather not.

- Don't play designer: Resist the temptation to use your word processor's bells and whistles. For italics, use underlines. In subheadings, use NO underlines unless italics are mandatory, for example, for genus and species. *Reason*: The copyeditor will have to write tedious instructions to the compositor to ignore (or observe) your italics and to delete or re-mark items for which the designer's instructions or house style differ.

- Keep all elements separate: Don't run tables, boxes, or drawings into the text proper. Designate where they are to go and put them at the end with separate numbers for each element (T2–1, T2–2, F-l, F-2, etc.). *Reason*: These elements are typeset separately from the text, often by a different person. Usually, figure captions are best typed separately, not on the figures themselves, for the same reason.

- Don't rule tables except (1) between column headings and table body and (2) at the bottom. *Reason*: It will take your typist an inordinate amount of time to put them in and your copy editor time to take them out. Trust me. Exception: matrix cells and the like.

- Be generous in changing ribbons on your printer. If you think "it'll do," it won't.

- Don't write on the copy-edited manuscript. That said, if you absolutely must insert something instead of using a flag or a separate sheet, do it in a bright color different from what the copy editor used and mark (with a 3M flag or whatever) every place where you have made a change. *Reason*: Insertions have to be edited. Yes—they do; 9.5 out of 10 authors insert style inconsistencies as well as misspellings and grammatical errors, often pertaining to something before or after the insertion.

- Don't erase or cross out the edit. Write "stet" [over the lines] ... and put little dots under the lines you want reinstated. *Reason*: See above. Also, the manuscript should be a permanent record of copy editor changes and your responses. If you insist on being wrong (or at least different), the copy editor should not later be blamed.

Proofreading

After you finish checking the copyedited manuscript and return it to the production editor, the manuscript will be typeset. The first proofs that you will be asked to check will be either galley or page ones. If they are galley proofs, they will be on sheets that are longer than 11 inches and most will contain more lines of type than can be placed on a single page. After you finish checking the galley proofs and return them, any typographical or other errors that you identified are corrected—at least theoretically. The lines of type are then removed from the galleys and combined with illustrations to form pages. Proofs will be made of the pages and you will be asked to check them. Incidentally, it is not safe to assume that all of the errors that you identified in the galleys were corrected. Check the page proofs carefully to make certain that all of them were corrected!

Up until the early 1990s, almost all book publishers had authors check both galley and page proofs. Now, it is fairly common for the first set of proofs that an author sees to be pages. This change may have been due at least partially to the fact that typesetting during this decade was increasingly done utilizing an author's word-processor files rather than printouts of them.

One or more proofreaders will compare the proofs to the copyedited manuscript and will correct typesetting errors on them. It is almost impossible to typeset a book without making some errors. When you are asked to read and correct the proofs, pay particular attention to facts, dates, statistics, spelling, and punctuation. Verify each illustration reference for correct positioning in the text. Also mark your corrections on the duplicate set of proofs (if one is provided) or photocopy the set after you have written your corrections on them. This is for "insurance" if the original is lost. Use standard proof correction notation (Appendix E). If the set you receive has been read and corrected by a proofreader, use a different color pencil for your corrections. The production editor will indicate any errors you found that the proofreader(s) missed and any wording changes you made on the master set of proofs and return them to the typesetter for correction. He or she will make the corrections indicated—at least theoretically.

You may receive the page proofs for the front matter (title page, table of contents, preface, etc.) with the others or later. Be certain to check carefully the spelling of your name and affiliation and the names and affiliations of those whom you've acknowledged.

When you return the page proofs to your production editor, he or she will add your corrections to the master set that was checked by the proofreader(s). When all the errors that were *found* are corrected, a high quality set of proofs (referred to as "repros") will be made. These will be photographed to create the plates for printing the book. The word "found" was italicized because there are likely to be errors that will not be spotted until after the book is published. You should report any you find (or are found by your students) to your acquisitions editor. They can be corrected in future reprintings and editions of the book (assuming, of course, that it sells enough copies for there to be some).

Checking the Cover Text

The design for the cover and dust jacket (if your book will have a dust jacket) will be created by a graphic designer, probably a freelance one. While you are unlikely to be consulted about visual aspects of the design, you are likely to be asked to check the text in it for accuracy. If you have suggestions for the design on either the cover or dust jacket of your book, mention them to your acquisitions editor prior to or immediately following the launch meeting. I have influenced the design on the cover of two of my books by doing so.

Indexing

After you return the corrected page proofs to your production editor, you will begin your last major responsibility—preparing the index. The quality of the index can significantly affect your book's sales (particularly if it is a textbook). Although you can arrange to have your book indexed by a freelance indexer (most charge between $2.00 and $3.00 a page—charges tend to be higher on the West Coast than on the East Coast), it is not advisable to do so unless you can find one who is very knowledgeable about the topics dealt with in your book. You may find it helpful, if you do decide not to index the book yourself, to consult the *Register of Indexers*, which is published annually by the American Society of Indexers. Your acquisitions or production editor, of course, may be able to recommend an indexer. Be aware, however, that unless it states in your contract that the publisher will pay for indexing, the amount the indexer charges will either have to be paid by you when the index is completed or it will be paid by the publisher and withheld from your future royalty income. This is another reason why it would be advantageous for you to do your index yourself. I have indexed all of my books. Even though I don't find indexing to be a particularly enjoyable activity, I do get pleasure from knowing that my books probably have more useful indexes than they would have had otherwise.

You will be expected to begin the index immediately after you finish checking the page proofs and will probably have about a month to complete it. Your production editor should be able to tell you after the launch meeting when you will be expected to do it. If you know you will not have adequate time to work on it when you are scheduled to do so, let your production editor know as soon as possible so that the production schedule can be adjusted.

You may or may not be required to prepare an author index in addition to a subject one. That is, the publisher may leave it up to you whether to prepare an author index. If your book is a text and you are not required to prepare an author index, you may choose to do so for a reason other than the usual ones. Having an author index can increase adoptions if you cite the research of persons who teach the course for which the book is intended. Some professors want students to be aware of their research and they, therefore, would prefer to adopt a text in which it is cited.

There is special software for indexing. The American Society of Indexers' publication *Guide to Indexing Software* evaluates software available for IBM personal computers and compatibles. It is not necessary, however, to use such software. Any word-processing program that has a "find" command can be used for indexing. The first time you refer to an item, you enter it in the index file at the appropriate point alphabetically. Whenever you have to refer to it again, you use the "find" function to locate it quickly. To date, I have indexed five books in this way.

I have found an efficient way to use this "find" command strategy to create an author index. I use the reference list in my copy of the copyedited manuscript to create the alphabetical author list for the index. When I see a particular author's name on a page proof, I use the "find" command to locate the name in the author index file and add the page number to the ones that follow it.

If your book is not a first edition, the index from the current edition can be quite useful for indexing it, particularly if you have it on a computer file. If you do, your first task is to delete items in it that are not relevant to or accurate for the new edition, including page numbers. I have used my word processor's "find and replace" command to delete page numbers. I simply ask the program to "find" each of the 10 digits from 0 to 9 and to "replace" each digit with nothing—that is, I would put nothing in the "replace" entry space. Consequently, the "find and replace" command would be issued 10 times—once for each of the 10 digits. After doing this, there would be a series of commas after each item in the index. Each of these commas would be separated from the next one by a space. To delete these commas and spaces I would use the "find and replace" command to locate each instance of " ," (i.e., space, comma) and replace it with nothing (i.e., I wouldn't keyboard anything in the "replace" space). The processes described in this paragraph will probably take less than 30 minutes.

The index will be typeset in pages after you send the diskette containing the file(s) for it and a printout to your production editor. You may be asked to check the proofs. This ordinarily is your last production-related responsibility.

If your project is a book, it will now be printed and bound. If it is a professional or educational material that will not be marketed in book form, it will be printed and packaged. Your production or acquisitions editor will probably send you one of the first copies that he or she receives from the bindery. You will receive your other "author copies" later from your publisher's distribution center.

One final comment. Don't be surprised if a few days after you receive the first copy of your book or material you experience some depression. Many of the authors whom I interviewed reported doing so. I have also. There can be several reasons. One is family, friends, and/or colleagues may respond less enthusiastically than you expected to your book being published. Another is grieving. Whenever you sustain a loss, you go through the grieving process—one stage of which is depression. You lost an activity—working on a book or other project—that added something to your life. Several of my interviewees reported that they dealt with their grieving by taking on another project. Doing so, of course, is not necessary. You are highly likely to arrive at the final stage of the process—"acceptance"—regardless of whether you take on another project.

ADDITIONAL PRODUCTION RESPONSIBILITIES WHEN SELF-PUBLISHING

If you intend to self-publish a book, the tasks required to create and produce it are the same as those described in this chapter. However, you will be responsible for more of them. Your added responsibilities will include those of a production editor. They also may include some production tasks, such as page design and typesetting. I will only provide an overview here of these tasks. A number of "how to" books for self-publishers describe in detail how to do them, including the following: Applebaum (1988), Brownstone and Frank (1985), Burgett (1989), Henderson (1980), Holt (1985), Kelper (1990), Miles (1987), Mueller (1978), Poynter (1989), and *Pressing Business: An Organizational Manual for Independent Publishers* (1984). The book by Poynter (1989) is generally regarded as the best source for practical information about all aspects of self-publishing.

Page design and typesetting can be done from the book's word-processor files, using either a desktop publishing program or a word-processing one that has this capability (e.g., Microsoft Word). Pages can either be printed with a laser or inkjet printer. Although one that prints at 300–360 dots per inch is acceptable for text and line drawings, one that does so at 600 or more dots per inch will produce pages that look more like those in professionally typeset books. The text and line drawings on pages printed at 1,200 or more dots per inch should look identical to those in high-quality typeset books. You can have the final drafts of your pages (your "camera-ready copy") printed at a copy shop or service bureau on a printer that prints 1,200 or more dots per inch. Have a few sample pages printed by this printer before you begin typesetting pages because the amount of material that will appear on a page printed by it may not be identical to that printed on a page by your computer printer.

Camera-ready copy for pages containing photographs should be printed at 2,400 dots per inch. The quality of photographs on pages printed at fewer dots per inch is unlikely to be very high.

If your book doesn't contain photographs and you want to print the camera-ready copy with your inkjet or laser printer, there is a trick you may be able to use to increase quality. It is to print the camera-ready copy larger than the page size in your book. When the printer reduces it (photographically), the number of dots per inch will increase. Printers ordinarily do not charge more for doing this. If your book pages are 6" × 9" or smaller, printing proofs on 8½" × 11" sheets and having them reduced photomechanically to 75 percent or less can yield a resolution of 400 dots per inch or greater. A resolution of 400 dots per inch is adequate for some books, particularly ones that do not contain very small type and are purchased by professionals primarily because they contain information that is useful to them.

The next step is to have the book printed and bound. There are several ways you can do this. Some are considerably more expensive than others. The one that is likely to be the cheapest is having the pages printed on 11" × 17" signatures (i.e., each would contain four 8½" × 11" pages) and having the book *perfect bound* with a printed wrap-around cover. Both the printing and binding could be done at a copy shop (e.g., Kinkos). Perfect binding is the standard glued-on cover you see on most paperbacks. The signatures are folded into pages, stacked, and roughened and then the cover is wrapped around and glued on. Perfect binding will present a squared-off spine on which the title and name of the author can be printed if the book contains at least 100 pages. Using this approach, it may be practical to have a first printing of as few as 100 copies.

If you are confident that you can sell at least 1,000 copies of your book, you may want to have it printed and bound by a firm that offers these services to commercial publishers. A book that is printed and bound by such a firm will look like a commercially published one. The pages can be printed in any of the standard book sizes, and they can either be perfect bound or case bound. The latter is the standard binding used for hardcover books. Although case binding is more expensive than perfect binding, the difference in cost between them is surprisingly little. There are listings of firms that are willing to perform these services for self-publishers in Applebaum (1988) and Poynter (1989).

The process for producing books that has been described here—printing them on sheets of paper and binding the sheets—is not the only possible one. They can, for example, be distributed as a series of word-processor files that readers can either print with their computer or read on their computer monitor. The files can be distributed on diskettes or downloaded from a site on the Internet. This form of publication is more practical for professional books than for textbooks. The main advantage of this approach is that no money has to be invested upfront for printing and binding.

There are three things you should do before printing your book. The first is to set up a publishing company having a name other than yours (mine is Codi Publications). Doing so is neither difficult nor expensive (see Poynter, 1989, for detailed how-to information). Reviewers are more likely to react positively to your book if the fact it is self-published isn't obvious. The second is to apply for a copyright. There are detailed instructions for doing this in Novick and Chasen (1984). And the third is to apply for an ISBN (International Standard Book Number). This is an international book identification system that is used by bookstores for ordering. There is a different ISBN for each edition of a book. The number is printed on both the copyright page and the back cover. See Poynter (1989) for information about applying for an ISBN.

7

How Textbooks and Other Educational and Professional Books and Materials Are Marketed

Quality of marketing is one of the most important determinants of the success of a textbook or other educational or professional book or material. It was the consideration that a group of 350 college textbook authors (surveyed by Publishing Directions in 1991) indicated was the most important when selecting a publisher. Regardless of whether your book or material is commercially published or self-published, persons who could benefit from reading it will have to be made aware of its existence and content. While it may seem reasonable to assume that any publisher will do whatever is necessary to make potential purchasers aware of the existence and content of the books and materials it publishes, this is not a safe assumption to make. Approximately a third of the group of 350 college textbook authors in one survey considered the marketing efforts to have been insufficient for at least one of their books.

Although authors' beliefs that their publishers have not made a "good faith" effort to market their books are often erroneous, it is nevertheless true both that publishers differ with regard to how they market their books and that a publisher is likely to have a larger marketing budget for some of the books and materials that it publishes than it does for others. As I have indicated elsewhere, decisions on marketing are made before a book or material is published, based on an estimate of its potential to be a "best seller" (e.g., to gain a relatively large share of the text market for a particular course). Unfortunately, the decision that a book or material is unlikely to become a "best seller" can result in a self-fulfilling prophesy—that is, it can cause relatively little to be invested in marketing it, thereby making it less likely to become a "best seller" than it would have been otherwise.

Let's assume that you choose a publisher with a good track record for marketing projects similar to yours in your field. In order to ensure that your project gets its fair share of your publisher's marketing resources, you should attempt to convince your acquisitions editor and your publisher's marketing manager that it has the potential to become a "best seller" (unless, of course, you really don't believe that it has this potential—e.g., it is a scholarly monograph)—and that you are willing to do your fair share to have it become one. That is, you should do whatever you can to make both your acquisitions editor and marketing manager aware of the actual size of the market for your book or material and to view you as a willing and helpful participant in the marketing process. There are suggestions in this chapter for doing both.

One of the main ways that authors can acquaint their acquisitions editor and marketing manager with the potential market for their book or material is through their responses to questions in the *marketing questionnaire* that all educational, scholarly, and professional book publishers require their authors to fill out. If you fill the questionnaire out both thoughtfully and candidly, you will not only provide your publisher with essential information, but your acquisitions editor and marketing manager will view you as someone who is willing to become involved with marketing the book or material—a real collaborator.

Many textbook and professional book authors avoid becoming involved with the marketing of their books. One reason, perhaps the main one, is what Applebaum and Evans (1978, p. 130) have termed a "fear of hustling":

> Authors rarely lobby for their books within the houses that publish them, and they're even less likely to go out by themselves in search of sales. Somehow, they seem to think, it's not dignified to hustle for anything you yourself create. Well, dignified people do it and for a dignified reason: believing what they have to say is worth saying, they accept the responsibility of finding those individuals who will benefit from being exposed to it.

Making people aware of the existence and content of a book or material you created that can be helpful to them is not only an academically and professionally respectable thing to do but also a decent thing to do.

MARKETING STRATEGIES USED BY PUBLISHERS

Some of the strategies that publishers use most often for marketing textbooks and other educational and professional books and materials are described in this section. Almost all of them can be used for marketing self-published books.

Listings in *Books in Print,* Catalogs, and Sites on the World Wide Web

One marketing strategy your publisher is almost certain to use if your project is a book is listing it in *Books in Print.* This is the "bible" used by bookstores and libraries for ordering books and by readers for locating ones that deal with particular topics.

Another marketing strategy that your publisher is likely to use is listing (and possibly describing) your book or material in its catalog(s). These may be sent to libraries as well as people in the fields in which it specializes.

Most educational and professional book and material publishers now have sites on the World Wide Web. Almost all of them contain an on-line catalog in which their "in print" books and materials are described and from which they can be ordered.

Soliciting Reviews in Professional Journals

Copies of your book or material will be sent to the review editors of at least some of the professional journals in your field. You will be asked in the author's questionnaire to suggest ones to which they should be sent. There, of course, is no guarantee that reviews will be published. Most journals lack sufficient space to review all of the books and materials that they receive.

You may also want to suggest journals to which review copies should not be sent. It is risky, for example, to request reviews from journals that do not give authors an opportunity to respond to negative reviews. While most books and materials that receive negative reviews deserve them, a book or material can receive a negative review for one or more of the following reasons: the reviewer did not understand the purpose of the book or material; the reviewer disagreed with some positions taken by the author; the reviewer disliked the author; or the reviewer is a "young Turk" who is attempting to build a reputation by taking on the establishment.

If your book or material receives a negative review in an influential journal and you are not given an opportunity by the review editor to respond, there are two ways that you may be able to partially undo the harm that the review did. One is to publish a response in the journal as a "letter to the editor." You should only do this if you can respond to the reviewer's criticisms cogently. If you don't respond to them, some persons are likely to assume that you could have if you had been given the opportunity to do so. On the other hand, if you respond and do it poorly or sound defensive, you are likely to lose them also. An alternative that is practical for some textbooks is mailing a response (along with a cover letter) to potential users. In my field (speech pathology) this would involve mailing them to about 225 training programs. I did this once and it seemed to work, judging by telephone calls and letters I received and subsequent sales.

Displaying the Book or Material at Professional Meetings

Another strategy that textbook and professional book and material publishers use for marketing their publications is displaying and selling them in the exhibit area at annual conventions of professional/scientific associations. Other ways they may market them at such conventions are by scheduling "meet the author" sessions at their booth and having an open house at a nearby hotel, during which interested persons can meet informally with their authors.

When you do a presentation at a professional meeting at which your publisher is not exhibiting, arrange with the firm to have an author's brochure (i.e., a sheet describing the book or material with an order form) and a copy or two of your book or material there for attendees to examine. You can distribute the brochure with your other handouts. If your publisher does not create an author's brochure for you, you can produce one yourself.

Advertising the Book or Material in Professional Journals

Another strategy that publishers sometimes use for marketing their publications—particularly their most recent ones—is advertising them in professional journals. In advertisements for textbooks, instructors are likely to be encouraged to request an examination copy. And in those for professional books and materials, ordering information is provided and purchasers may be allowed to order "on approval." Journal advertising tends to be expensive, and I have been told by several acquisitions editors that it often doesn't produce enough sales to justify the expenditure.

Direct-Mail Advertising

Some form of direct-mail advertising probably will be used to promote your book or material. It may be the only one mentioned in a particular mailing or it may be one of several. It is likely to be the latter because it costs publishers less to promote their products in this way.

You probably will be asked in the author's questionnaire to suggest groups to whom direct-mail advertising should be sent. If your book or material is a professional one, you will be asked for the names of organizations to which working professionals who are likely to be interested in it belong. For a textbook, you will be asked for the titles of courses for which it would be appropriate. You may also be asked for a list of schools that offer such courses.

Distributing Examination Copies

One of the main strategies publishers use for marketing college textbooks is distributing examination copies. They may send a copy to all the people they know who teach a particular course or only to those who request one after hearing about it by "word of mouth," seeing an advertisement, reading a review, receiving a direct-mail piece, examining a copy at a professional meeting, and/or being contacted by one of the publisher's sales representatives. Those who receive an examination copy may not be charged for it whether or not they adopt the book or, perhaps, only if their bookstore orders a certain number of copies (e.g., 10 or more). If a publisher has the latter policy, examination copies will only be sent to persons who request them, and those who decide not to adopt the book will be allowed to either return or purchase it.

Contacting Potential Adopters in Person or by Telephone

One of the main marketing strategies used by textbook publishers is having their representatives contact and make a "sales pitch" to potential adopters. Traditionally, local sales representatives visit them at their offices. Some publishers are now using telemarketing for making such contacts and sales pitches, particularly for texts for upper-division undergraduate and graduate courses. They still may use face-to-face representative contact for potential adopters of texts for large-enrollment, lower-division undergraduate courses. A person who had been the president of the college textbook division of a major book publisher that used telemarketing for this purpose told me that the company's internal research indicated that the telemarketing approach yielded more adoptions than the direct contact one. This should not be particularly surprising. A representative can contact more potential adopters in a day by telephone than by traveling from campus to campus and from office to office on a campus. A representative who fails to find a potential adopter in his or her office probably will have to wait at least a few months to again attempt to reach him or her. On the other hand, one who is unable to contact a potential adopter when he or she phones can call back later that day or the next.

Regardless of whether a publisher's sales representatives contact potential adopters in person or by telephone, it is desirable to communicate with the representatives by e-mail or "snail mail" to facilitate their "bonding" both to you and to your book. If they know you as a person rather than merely as a name in their sales book or catalog, they are likely to try harder to market your book to potential adopters, particularly if it isn't one for a large-enrollment undergraduate course. And if they develop real enthusiasm for your book, they are also more likely to make a real effort to market it. You can provide them with information about the book that will help them to market it, including suggestions for responding to specific concerns about it that potential adopters may mention. If your communication with them does nothing else, it will keep you and your book on their mind ("out of sight, out of mind"), which is likely to result in a greater effort to market it and, hopefully, a larger number of adoptions.

Selling Publication Rights or Books to Professional Book Clubs

A strategy that some publishers use for marketing upper-division undergraduate- and graduate-level textbooks to working professionals is selling copies (or the right to print them) to professional book clubs. There is at least one for most fields. For example, those that are man-

aged by Newbridge Book Clubs—at the time this chapter was written—include the following: Architects & Designers Book Service,
Astronomy Book Club, Behavioral Science Book Service, Instructor's
Pre-School Book Club, The Library of Computer and Information Sciences, The Library of Science, The Library of Special Education, The
Library of Speech-Language Pathology, Natural Science Book Club,
The Nurse's Book Society, and The Teacher Book Club. Others are
listed in the book *Literary Market Place*. If the right to print a certain
number of copies rather than actual books is sold, the author receives a
percentage of the money paid to the publisher (e.g., 50 percent) rather
than a royalty. Some professional book and material publishers also sell
to other kinds of book clubs.

Selling Publication Rights to Foreign Publishers

Most educational and professional book and material publishers will
attempt to sell their products in other countries if they believe that there
is an international market for them. There are several ways they may do
this. One is to arrange for publishers in other English-speaking countries (or their own subsidiaries in them) to publish the book or material
jointly. It will be copyrighted in these countries as well as in the United
States. The royalty percentage for such sales may be lower than the
usual bookstore one. Another is to sell translation rights. A publisher
buys the right to translate a book or material into a particular language
and print an edition of a particular size. Such rights sales are handled
similarly to those for book clubs—that is, the author receives a percentage of the money paid to the publisher.

Offering Ancillaries

A strategy that publishers sometimes use for marketing textbooks—particularly ones for introductory courses—is offering ancillaries (i.e., materials that facilitate teaching the course) to instructors who
adopt them. Those offered could include sets of multiple-choice test
questions, suggestions for class activities, slides, overhead transparencies, audio tapes, videotapes, sites on the World Wide Web, and/or
computer software. A publisher is most likely to offer ancillaries if the
publishers of competing texts do so. If none currently offer them, it
may be possible to increase adoptions by doing so. Teachers of introductory college courses, for example, are likely to appreciate sets of

multiple-choice test questions. If your editor is unwilling to have ancillaries created for your book because doing so would be too expensive, he or she may be willing to reproduce and distribute ones that you create.

MARKETING SELF-PUBLISHED BOOKS

Our focus thus far has been on strategies that commercial publishers use for marketing textbooks and professional books. You can use the same ones if you self-publish. As I have previously indicated, if you publish under a company name rather than your own, your book is not likely to be regarded as having been self-published. The books by Applebaum (1988), Holt (1985), Kremer (1990), and Poynter (1989) provide specific suggestions for marketing self-published books.

WHAT YOU CAN DO

To judge whether your publisher's plan for marketing (promoting) your book or material is likely to be adequate, you first have to know what it is. You can get this information from your publisher's marketing manager—the person who plans the advertising, promotion, and marketing campaign for your book or material—by asking a series of questions, such as the following ones that were adapted from a list suggested by Dudley Kay in a presentation at the 1989 Text and Academic Authors Association convention. Even though this list was intended for textbooks, most of the items in it are relevant to other educational and professional books and materials as well.

- What exactly will be mailed to instructors? When?
- Will you prepare an author's brochure on my book that I can distribute as a handout when I give presentations?
- In what journals might my book be advertised? When?
- Will my book be promoted by direct mail? To whom?
- Will other books be promoted with mine in journal advertisements and direct-mail pieces? [The fewer, the better.]
- To what journals will review copies be sent?
- At what conventions will it be displayed?
- Are comparative marketing reviews being commissioned?
- What sales support items are being prepared?

- Will a reader's [response] card be enclosed with comps [complimentary copies]?
- May I see a printout of comps sent to instructors?
- What follow-up will be sent to instructors comped?
- What follow-up will be sent to instructors *not* comped?
- Will my book be promoted internationally? How exactly? Is my book a candidate for an international paperback edition?
- Is my book being submitted for translations? Who handles?
- Will my book be submitted to _____ book club(s)?
- Will my book be offered to any mail order catalog houses?
- Will my book be promoted outside colleges? How exactly?
- Who will promote my book at sales meetings? May I speak to the sales representatives at national or regional meetings?
- May I write a letter/memo to the sales representatives?
- Will my book be sent to *Choice* for review? [For college libraries.]
- Can I buy my book at standard reseller discount (30–35 percent) and sell it myself?
- HOW CAN I HELP? HOW CAN I HELP? HOW CAN I HELP?

By merely asking these questions, you are communicating that you know how your book should be marketed. This could motivate the marketing manager, who is the holder of the promotion budget purse strings, to do more to promote it than he or she would have otherwise.

If you believe that the marketing plan for your book or material isn't adequate, what can you do? The first thing is to communicate your concerns to the marketing manager and/or your acquisitions editor along with specific suggestions for improving it that are likely to be doable. Your presentation should be well reasoned (rather than emotional) and should be communicated in a letter rather than a telephone conversation. The individual you contact probably is going to have to get the permission of at least one person to have the marketing plan changed. If you present your concerns and suggestions in a letter, he or she may be able to communicate them more accurately than if doing so requires paraphrasing a telephone conversation. If you argue your case cogently and make suggestions that are doable, you should be able to at least partially achieve your goal. Anyway, it seems to be worth trying, judging by the following comment by Judith Applebaum and Nancy Evans that was printed in the masthead of the *Authors Guild Bulletin* for January-February 1978: "Persuading your publisher to get out there and sell your book is a never-ending job that demands a great deal of gall. . . . Publishing people all admit that the more an author nags, the more attention his [or her] book gets." If the individual you contact argues that the plans for marketing your book are adequate, this may be true. You should be as open-minded to his or her arguments as you expect he or she to be to yours.

There are things you may be able to do to augment the marketing plan for your book or material. Obviously, the more people there are who are aware it exists, the more there are who are likely to purchase it. Consequently, anything you can do to increase awareness of it is likely to result in increased sales. One way you can do this is by mentioning the book or material in oral convention and workshop presentations (possibly including an author's brochure in the handout) and in journal articles. It is crucial that you do it in a way that is not likely to cause you to be perceived as being unprofessional.

One strategy you can use for marketing a textbook prior to its publication is to request reviews of chapters (or the entire manuscript) from persons who are in a position to adopt it or recommend its adoption. This could cause them to make an "ego investment" in the book. Their assistance should be acknowledged in the preface. Everything else being equal, instructors would be more likely to adopt and recommend books in which they had input than ones in which they did not.

Perhaps, as I have indicated previously, the one thing you can do prior to publication that is most likely to result in an adequate marketing plan for your book or material is to give a great deal of thought to your responses to items in the author's questionnaire. For example, suggestions you make for publications to which review copies should be sent and members of organizations to whom brochures should be mailed are likely to be taken seriously. Also, if your book is a textbook, comments that you make about how it differs from the competition are likely to be distributed to the publisher's field representatives and communicated by them to potential adopters. In fact, you may want to attach a formal feature-need-benefit analysis (see Figure 4.1).

The things you can do after publication to augment efforts to market your book or material include the following:

- If your book or material should be of interest to teachers or working professionals in your field in a country in which the national language isn't English, send complimentary copies to several who live in this country who are likely to have contact with a publisher who publishes books or materials for professionals in it. Your publisher may be willing to give you a few copies to use for this purpose. Even if the outcome isn't a foreign-language edition, it could still be worthwhile—for example, you could receive an invitation to participate in an international meeting for which the organizing committee will pay at least part of your travel expenses.

- Send your acquisitions editor and marketing manager copies of letters you receive in which complimentary comments are made about the book or material, particularly ones from persons who are well known and respected in your field. Your publisher may be able to use them for promoting the book.

- If it is a college textbook, write an article for one of your national association's journals or do an oral presentation at its national convention in which you present your point of view about how the course for which the book is intended should be taught. Instructors who agree with your point of view are likely to give serious consideration to adopting your book.

- If your book is a college textbook and your publisher has a representative who visits faculty at local colleges and universities, it is worthwhile to contact the person and try to get him or her enthusiastic about your book. Doing so, of course, can increase sales locally. It also can increase them nationally because his or her enthusiasm about the book can be communicated to other local representatives at regional and national sales meetings.

- To encourage your publisher to market your book by direct mail when there appears to be no plan to do so, you may want to prepare a set of mailing labels and send them to the marketing manager. I was successful in getting a publisher to do so in this way.

- If you have written a textbook, you might want to write, e-mail, or phone some potential adopters to ask if they have received an examination copy and indicate that you would appreciate any suggestions that they or their students would care to make for improving the next edition. This is a way to alert potential adopters to the availability of the book without making yourself appear to be a huckster.

- If you have written a textbook that contains a comprehensive bibliography of an aspect of a field, another way to alert faculty to the book's availability without appearing to be a huckster is to write to chairpersons of departments in the field and ask them to encourage members of their faculty who are publishing in it to send you copies of their relevant journal publications and convention presentations for future updates of the bibliography. Enclose a sheet describing the book on which there is an order form. If this strategy doesn't result in an adoption, it is at least likely to result in a single copy sale to the institution's library because comprehensive bibliographies are generally regarded as being useful "tools."

- If you have written a book that is of interest to working professionals in your field, you might want to try to arrange with your publisher to conduct a "meet the author book signing" at its booth at your national convention. Your publisher, of course, must be willing to have copies available for sale at its booth.

- If you have written a book that is of interest to the general public, you may want to arrange for live or telephone appearances on local radio talk shows. You may also want to arrange for signing sessions at bookstores. Your publisher may be willing to reimburse some of your travel expenses. It does no harm to ask!

For additional suggestions of ways that you can assist your publisher in marketing (promoting) your book or material, see Kremer (1990).

MARKETING AN "OUT OF PRINT" BOOK

Eventually your publisher will declare your book out of print. If your publisher does so while you believe there is still a market for the book, there are at least two ways can you keep it in print. If your publisher still has some copies and agrees to sell them to you at low cost and return the copyright, you can self-publish the book and have it listed in *Books in Print* under the name of your firm. Another way is to use an out-of-print book publishing service, such as that offered by University Microfilms International (300 North Zeeb Road, Ann Arbor, Michigan 28106). You can list your book with them at no cost and you will receive a 10 percent royalty on every book sold. All they will need from you is one copy of the book since they will use a xerographic process for reproducing it. There was a somewhat similar service being offered on the Internet—when this chapter was written—that sold books as downloadable files that could be viewed on a monitor or printed by the purchaser.

Suppose that when your book is declared out of print it needs to be revised (updated) before being republished. If the copyright has been returned to you, you can seek a contract from another publisher for a revised edition or a new book that contains much of the material in it. I have kept two of my books in print this way. Or you can revise the book and self-publish it.

8

Tax and Other Business Implications of Authorship

Authoring books and materials for which there is a *profit motive* is regarded by the government—including the IRS—as operating a small business. The various municipal, state, and federal laws that regulate such businesses are applicable to authorship. Some obligations that are imposed by and opportunities that arise from it being classified in this way are discussed in this chapter, along with several other business-related implications of authorship.

TAX IMPLICATIONS

The words "profit motive" in the preceding paragraph are italicized for an important reason. This is the criterion the IRS uses to differentiate authorship that is a hobby from that which is a business. The IRS considers authorship to be a business (when this chapter was written) if some tax is paid on income three out of five years—that is, if income exceeds expenses this frequently. If the IRS regards you as having a profit motive, you will be allowed certain deductions that you will not be allowed otherwise, particularly ones that result in your declaring a loss that can be deducted from your other income.

The IRS will sometimes classify a business as having a profit motive even if it doesn't generate income three out of five years. If, for example, you have a contract from an established publisher and there are four years between the date you sign the contract and the date that you receive your first royalty check, you can still deduct most of your authoring-related expenses from your other income the year that they occur. However, you may be asked by the IRS to explain why your "business" is declaring a loss more than three out of five years. If this happens, you can use your publishing contract as documentation for your having a profit motive.

Assuming that you report your income on IRS Form 1040 (U.S. Individual Income Tax Return), you would use Schedule C (Profit and Loss from Business) for reporting income and expenses from authorship. If you are not self-publishing, your income from it will consist of advances and royalty payments. If you are doing so, it will consist of income received from the sale of books.

There are a number of types of expenses "proximately related" (language used by the IRS) to authorship that the IRS will allow you to deduct from income. However, to do so you must be able to document them. The IRS says that the records you use for this purpose must be "permanent, accurate, complete, and must clearly establish income [and] deductions." Furthermore, they should be retained until the statute of limitations for that return expires, which is ordinarily three years after the return was due to be filed or two years after the date the tax was paid, whichever occurs later. For capital equipment, such as a microcomputer or camera, that you are recovering the cost of over a period of years by depreciation, you should hold on to the receipt for as long as you own the article.

The following are some suggestions for documenting expenses. Retain receipts for all deductible items for which you either pay cash or use a charge card. If you are claiming business-related car mileage, keep a detailed diary of dates, destinations, and mileages. You can purchase a special log book at an office supply store to keep in your car for documenting these. Also, pay deductible expenses by check whenever possible. You should consider establishing a separate checking account for this purpose, especially if you are self-publishing. Canceled checks usually are accepted by the IRS as prima facie evidence of an expense.

The kinds of expenses that are "proximately related" to authorship and that the IRS usually will allow to be deducted from income on Schedule C include the following:

Advertising

Included here would be expenses for advertising/marketing your book or material if it is self-published or for assisting in doing so if it is not self-published.

Bank Charges

If you have a separate checking account and/or safe deposit box for authoring business, the bank charges for it can be deducted.

Commissions

In the unlikely event that you have a literary agent, you can deduct commissions paid to him or her.

Depreciation

If you purchase equipment (e.g., a microcomputer) or furnishings (e.g., a desk) that can be expected to have a useful life of more than one year, you may not be able to deduct the total amount in the year you purchase it. Its cost may be recovered over the period of its "useful life." When this chapter was written, the IRS allowed up to $10,000 worth of equipment to be deducted in the year it was purchased if doing so did not push a profit into a loss. See the IRS *Tax Guide for Small Businesses* for information about this and the various ways depreciation can be computed.

Dues and Publications

The costs of books and journals that you purchase for researching your book as well as those you purchase to learn more about authoring and publishing (including this book) can be deducted. You can also deduct dues to writer's organizations, such as the Text and Academic Authors Association, and registration fees and travel expenses for attending their conventions and workshops.

Freight

You can deduct this if you self-publish your book or material and send shipments by freight to book dealers.

Insurance

The cost of insurance on equipment and furnishings used for authoring can be deducted. This would include a percentage of your homeowner's or renter's insurance if you claim a home-office deduction: You would report it—when this chapter was written—on IRS Form 8829 rather than Schedule C of Form 1040.

Interest on Business Indebtedness

If you borrow money to buy equipment or furniture for authoring, you can deduct the interest. This, of course, would apply to credit card interest.

Legal and Professional Services

If you hire an attorney to review your contract or for any other authorship-related purpose, you can write off this expense. You can also write off other professional expenses such as hiring an illustrator to draw figures.

Motor Vehicle Expenses

If you use your car while researching your book (e.g., for traveling to libraries), operating costs, parking fees, and other related expenses are deductible. This can be done either as a ratio of business use to total use or on a cost-per-business-mile basis as established annually by the IRS. The latter is probably less likely to result in an audit. Regardless of which method you use, keep accurate trip records. Most office supply stores sell log books for doing so.

Office in Your Home

If you own your home, have a room set aside that you use "regularly and exclusively" for your authoring activities, and can convince the IRS that you have a profit motive, you probably will be allowed to deduct the cost of maintaining this room even if you have an office at your place of employment. The percentage of your mortgage payment you can deduct is determined by the percentage of the square footage of your home that is devoted to the office. If the office is 150 square feet and your home is 1,500 square feet, you can deduct 10 percent. However, you can't use office-in-the-home expenses to push a profit into a loss. Expenses that can't be deducted because they would do so can be carried over to the following year (assuming that doing so wouldn't push a profit into a loss). The IRS has very strict rules about the office-in-the-home deduction and claiming it will increase the probability that your return will be audited. However, assuming you are able to convince the auditor that the room is used "regularly and exclusively" for your authoring activities and that you have a profit motive, the deduction should be allowed.

If you report income and expenses from authoring on Schedule C of the federal Form 1040 tax statement and include home-office deductions, you must itemize these expenses on Form 8829. For further information about IRS thinking concerning home offices, order the free IRS publication *Business Use of Your Home*.

Office Supplies

In addition to office supplies, you would include what you paid to have materials (including journal articles and drafts of your manuscript) photocopied. Also, if you purchased any inexpensive pieces of equipment, you may be able to deduct their cost here.

Postage

All authorship-related postage can be deducted, including that for obtaining research materials and mailing manuscripts and corrected galley and page proofs to the publisher.

Rent on Business Property

If you are renting your home or apartment and have set part of it aside *exclusively* for use as an office, you can deduct the appropriate portion of the rent. If you use it for other purposes as well, you cannot do so. Rental fees for special equipment (such as renting a computer by the hour at a copy shop) can also be deducted.

Repairs

The cost of repairs on the equipment and furnishings you use for authoring are deductible.

Taxes

Taxes related to authoring, such as sales taxes on equipment, can be deducted.

Telephone

If you have a separate telephone line for your authoring business, you can deduct the cost of it.

Travel and Entertainment

You can deduct authorship-related travel expenses here, such as those incurred when researching your book (e.g., traveling to another city to use a special library collection) or meeting with your acquisitions editor. You usually are not allowed to deduct expenses that fall into the category of commuting—that is, traveling from your home to work. The IRS has strict rules regarding travel and entertainment deductions. Ask for its publication dealing with them.

Utilities

If you have an office in your home, you can deduct an appropriate portion of the cost of utilities (see the "square footage" discussion in the office-in-the-home section). The safest way to deduct them (i.e., to minimize the likelihood of triggering an IRS audit) is to have separate meters for your office.

These are not the only business-related deductions allowed by the IRS. However, they are the ones that authors are most likely to take. Since the rules used by the IRS for determining which deductions are allowable change somewhat from year to year, you would be wise to consult with a tax expert to verify that the deductions mentioned here that you plan to take are still allowable. You may also want to consult with one to determine which of them are applicable to your state income tax.

Publishers do not withhold any money from advances or royalty checks for federal or state income taxes. Depending on the amount of profit you expect to make from authoring and the amount you and your employer have contributed to your social security account, you may have to make quarterly prepayments for income tax and/or social security using the 1040ES form. If your prepayments are too little, you may have to pay a penalty. One way that some authors avoid the hassle of making them is by having their employer increase the amount of tax withheld from their salary.

SOCIAL SECURITY AND OTHER BUSINESS IMPLICATIONS OF RETIREMENT

After you retire and begin collecting social security, your benefits will be reduced if you *earn* more than a certain amount. Your royalty income is likely to be viewed by the Social Security Administration as income you earned the year it was received. As a consequence, your benefits could be reduced either because your royalty income by itself exceeded the maximum you can earn without being penalized or your royalties in conjunction with your other income (e.g., salary from part-time teaching or consulting) exceeded this amount. I was informed by two professors who authored textbooks prior to their retirement that they were able to keep their royalty income from being classified as earned the year it was received by documenting when their books were written. If the copyright date on a book precedes the one on which you retired, it is relatively simple to document this. If the manuscript for a book was completed prior to your retiring but was published after your doing so, you should still be able to keep your royalty income from being classified as earned. A letter from your acquisitions editor acknowledging acceptance of your manuscript prior to the date you retired could be used to document when the book was written. For further information about this issue, contact the Social Security Administration office in your district.

Aside from social security, retirement can have other business implications for authors. Generating income from authorship may be more important to you after you retire than it was prior to your doing so.

WHEN TO INCORPORATE

Authoring, like all businesses, can have one of three organizational structures—a sole proprietorship, a partnership, or a corporation. The first—the *sole proprietorship*—is the least complex of these organizational forms and the one used by most authors. With it, the business is owned by one person—the author. More than half the businesses in this country are sole proprietorships. The owner may employ other persons—for example, a part-time secretary. Two advantages of individual ownership are that the owner is responsible only to himself or herself and reaps the profits if the enterprise is successful. One disadvantage of it is that the owner is entirely responsible for any debts that the business incurs. If the owner does not have sufficient funds to cover them, creditors could ask a court to order that his or her home and other possessions be sold.

Partnership differs from individual ownership in that the business is owned by two or more persons. Any number of persons can enter into a partnership. Those entering into one can invest their money or their time (services) or both. An author who self-publishes could have a partner who provides the upfront money for doing so. A contract, or agreement, usually is drawn up that specifies the rights and duties of all participants in the partnership. The partners share equally in both the profits and losses of the business unless the agreement specifies otherwise. If there are losses, the partners are obliged to pay them from personal funds. A partnership agreement may be for a limited or indefinite period of time.

One disadvantage of both sole proprietorship and partnership is that any losses incurred by a business have to be paid by its owner or owners. One advantage of the *corporate structure* is that it ordinarily protects the owner(s) from personal liability if there are losses. The reason is that a corporation is classified by the courts as a *person*—an independent entity. A corporation can buy and sell property in its own name, and it can commit crimes and be punished for them. Businesses established as sole proprietorships and partnerships are not regarded by the courts as independent entities but as extensions of their owners. Thus, the initiation of a court action against a sole proprietorship or partnership involves suing its owner or owners. The main disadvantage of the corporate structure is that the income generated does not belong to the owner and owners (it belongs to the entity—the corporation), and consequently, there are restrictions on how it can be spent. Income from a sole proprietorship or partnership can be used for any purpose.

It sometimes is advantageous for an author to incorporate. One reason is for liability protection. An author who is self-publishing or is at higher than normal risk for being sued (e.g., for libel) may decide to incorporate for this reason. Also, there can be tax advantages for doing so, particularly if you are planning to invest your royalty income in a retirement plan rather than using it for current expenses. A CPA can advise you about this.

ROYALTY STATEMENTS

Review your royalty statements carefully. In a presentation at an annual convention of the Text and Academic Authors Association, Paul Rosenzweig, a CPA knowledgeable about the publishing industry, suggested that the following set of questions be used as a guide when doing so:

- Are all the titles listed?
- Is each edition of every title listed?
- Are workbooks and other ancillary materials listed?
- If there was a price increase since the last royalty statement, is the new price point reflected?
- If you know of foreign sales, are they reflected on the statement? If they are, but at very low prices (high discount), find out how the sales were affected.
- If there have been reprintings, are reported sales sufficiently higher, reflecting the need to reprint?
- If returns are very high, or negative sales are reported, are reasons known?
- Are titles properly segregated, according to contract terms?
- Are the royalty rates correct?
- If the contract calls for step rates [e.g., 12.5 percent on the first 3,000 copies and 15 percent thereafter], are they in use on the royalty statement, and are they correctly applied?
- Are there any chargebacks to the author on the statement [e.g., for drawing figures], and do you agree with them?

If you believe that the number of books sold has been underestimated or some other error has been made, you should contact your publisher's royalty department. Mistakes sometimes occur. In a recent royalty statement, I was shortchanged more than a thousand dollars by a computer error! If after doing so, you still believe that you haven't received all the royalty income due you, you may want to arrange for an independent audit of your royalty account. However, having it done can be expensive. According to Linden (1992, p. 130): "Requiring somewhere between a few days and two weeks of a specialized accountant's time at up to $200 an hour, an audit can easily cost $5,000 or $10,000." You probably will have to pay for having it done unless the discrepancy between what you were paid and what was owed you is substantial.

There are CPAs who will do a royalty audit on a contingency fee basis if it looks promising enough. The CPA will retain a percentage of the amount that he or she recovers. A list of CPAs who do royalty audits on this basis can be obtained from the Text and Academic Authors Association.

PHONE CALLS TO YOUR PUBLISHER

Telephone calls that you make to your publisher—particularly ones to your acquisitions editor or production editor—can be expensive if your publisher does not have an 800 number for its editorial offices. Some publishers that do not have an 800 number will allow their editors to accept the charges for calls from their authors. I have saved hundreds of dollars during the past 25 years by phoning editors collect.

BRANCHING OUT

Some persons who author academic books or materials eventually branch out into other types of authoring and/or other activities for which their authoring gives them credibility. This branching out may occur either before or after they retire and may be done instead of or in addition to authoring academic books or materials. Some of the ways in which they have branched out are described here.

Conducting Workshops

One author whom I interviewed, who had been retired for several years, developed a workshop based on one of his books to maximize his income from authoring:

> If you have any gift for giving workshops, it is very helpful to write a book that you could use as part of a workshop. I did this and developed a brochure on the workshop that I sent to groups I thought might be interested. . . . From a retirement point of view, whatever your field, you ought to consider the possibility of supplementing your written work with workshops.

You could, of course, conduct workshops before retiring and have your book be part of the "package" covered by the registration fee. For further information about workshops and other ways you can sell the expertise that your book represents, see Burgett (1989).

Consulting and Serving as an Expert Witness

A person who has authored a successful academic book on a topic usually is regarded as being an expert on it—someone whose opinions about the topic have value. Such opinions could be of value, for example, to someone who is engaging in an activity for which the experience and advice of an expert makes it unnecessary for him or her to "reinvent the wheel." They could also be of value to someone who is involved in litigation. Persons who have authored successful academic books are sought by attorneys to serve as expert witnesses because the fact that they have authored them is likely to make juries regard their opinions as credible. For further information about serving as an expert witness, see Chapter 16 in Silverman (1992).

Producing Audiobook Versions of or Supplements for Academic Books

Some academic books may also be publishable in whole (or part) in audio tape versions. Students—particularly ones who are more "auditory" than "visual" minded—can use such tapes to learn terminology (vocabulary) and to review for exams. They can play them in their dorm rooms and/or in their cars' tape decks while they are driving. You will probably have to get the permission of your publisher to self-publish or have another publisher publish such an audiobook. For information about publishing audiobooks, contact the Audiobook Publishers Association (APA) at their Web site (www.audiopub.com).

Authoring Adult and/or Juvenile Nonfiction Books

Some academic authors branch out by writing nonfiction trade books on subjects related to their areas of expertise for children and/or adults. These books are designed to introduce a technical or other subject to persons in a particular age range who have little or no previous knowledge of it, and to do so in a way that will, hopefully, be both interesting and understandable to them. Rather than being printed books, they may be audiobooks or CD-ROM multimedia presentations.

Facilitating the Growth of Your Field in Developing Countries

If your books are known to persons in developing countries and if their level of development in your field is relatively low, you may be able to contribute to raising it by consulting, offering workshops, and/or serving as a visiting professor. This is one of the main ways that my books have enabled me to branch out. For information about and strategies for becoming involved internationally, see Silverman (1996).

Appendixes

APPENDIX A
A Representative Book Proposal

AUTHORING TEXTBOOKS AND OTHER ACADEMIC AND PROFESSIONAL BOOKS AND MATERIALS

Franklin H. Silverman, Ph.D.
Professor of Speech Pathology, Marquette University, Milwaukee, WI
   Clinical Professor of Rehabilitation Medicine, Medical College of Wisconsin, Wauwatosa, WI
President-Elect, Text and Academic Authors Association (TAA)

Textbooks and professional reference books are among the most important tools for facilitating the learning process. Many teachers and other professionals have "played with the idea" of authoring one. There is certain information that they need in order to make an informed decision about undertaking such a project and, if they decide to do so, to maximize the probability of being successful. This book will provide the information in a style that is both conversational and candid. Much of it will also be of interest to persons who have authored textbooks and/or professional reference books or who have created or are contemplating creating academic and professional materials other than printed books, including multimedia ones on CD-ROMs, computer software, audio tapes, videotapes, diagnostic tests, and educational materials.

This book is based on a six-hour workshop that I have been conducting annually for the past 10 years under the auspices of the Text and Academic Authors Association. The workshop has also been conducted under the auspices of several universities. Participants have included faculty from colleges and universities, junior colleges, high schools, middle schools, and elementary schools, as well as working professionals from a variety of fields. Some were working on or had completed a book project. Most, however, had an idea for a book, but did not know how to proceed. Specifically, they were seeking information about such aspects of authorship as the qualifications academic book publishers expect authors to possess, how they could be both "helped and hurt" by authoring an academic book, factors to consider when identifying potential publishers for this type of book, preparing a proposal, negotiating a contract, strategies that facilitate writing a manuscript and preparing illustrations for this type of book, authors' responsibilities during production (including indexing), authors' responsibilities for marketing their book, and business aspects of authorship (including tax ones). All of these topics and issues are dealt with as they apply to textbooks, professional books, and other types of educational materials.

The primary audience for the book is teachers—at all levels from nursery school to college. It could be marketed to them through college and trade bookstores. It could also be marketed to them by direct mail. For example, the membership lists of authoring groups such as the Text and Academic Authors Association and The Authors Guild could be used for this purpose. Also, advertisements could be placed in periodicals read by teachers, including the *Chronicle of Higher Education*. A secondary market for the book is libraries, including college libraries, municipal libraries, and professional libraries maintained by schools for their faculty. The book, if it is favorably reviewed, would be a "must buy" for college and university libraries, of which there are thousands. It would also be a "must buy" for larger municipal libraries. I have been authoring textbooks and professional reference books for more than 20 years and currently have six "in print." A fourth edition of one of them will be published later this year.

Contents (Tentative)

Preface

Chapter 1   **Qualifications Necessary for Authoring a Textbook, Professional Reference Book, or Other Educational Material**

One of the first decisions that a person has to make when contemplating authoring a textbook, professional reference book, or other educational material is deciding whether he or she has the qualifications necessary to successfully complete the project. Both the qualifications that people are likely to assume are necessary and really are (e.g., motivation) and those they are likely to assume are necessary but really aren't (e.g., being a recognized authority on the topic of the book and having large blocks of time available for writing) are discussed.

Chapter 2   **Potential Benefits and Losses: Financial and Other**

Prior to deciding whether to make any investment, you should identify the benefits and losses that could result from your doing so. Authoring a book (or creating another type of educational intellectual property) is making an investment. If the benefits from authoring are likely to outweigh the losses, then the investment may be worth making. A number of benefits that persons who author textbooks, professional reference books, and other educational materials may gain and the losses they may experience are described in this chapter.

Chapter 3   Choosing a Publisher

There are two publishing options for educational books and materials: doing it yourself (self-publishing) or having someone else do it. Advantages and disadvantages of each are described and a number of factors are indicated that academic authors should consider when selecting a publisher (assuming that they decide not to self-publish).

Chapter 4   Preparing a Proposal for an Academic Book and Other Type of Educational Material

Most publishing contracts for academic book and other educational material projects are awarded on the basis of a proposal and sample (e.g., a sample chapter or chapters). A number of factors that should be considered when defining the project and preparing the proposal package are discussed. The sample "successful" proposal package in Appendix A is used to illustrate aspects of this discussion.

Chapter 5   Negotiating a Contract for an Educational Book or Material Project and a Joint Collaboration Agreement

The standard publishing contract for an educational book or material contains a number of clauses. The implications of each of these clauses is explained and strategies for negotiating certain ones are described. [Academic authors usually negotiate their own contracts.] The need for joint collaboration agreements is discussed and the clauses that are usually included in them are described. A representative publishing contract and the joint collaboration agreement in Appendix B are referred to frequently.

Chapter 6   Creating an Educational Book or Material

Practical suggestions are provided for facilitating the various tasks needed to create an educational book or material. Some of these suggestions are from interviews with experienced authors. Practical suggestions also are provided for facilitating an author's production responsibilities. The results of the study, summarized in Appendix C, about textbook features that students do and don't find helpful are referred to frequently.

Chapter 7   **Marketing Responsibilities**

Academic authors are expected to participate in the marketing of their books and materials in several ways. These are described along with practical suggestions for meeting these responsibilities that are based, in part, on interviews with successful authors.

Chapter 8   **Tax and Other Business Aspects of Authorship**

Authoring books and other materials for which there is a "profit motive" is regarded by the government (including the IRS) as operating a small business. The various regulations that apply to such businesses are applicable to authorship. These regulations and other relevant business aspects of authorship are discussed in this chapter.

Appendix A **A Representative Book Proposal**

Appendix B **A Representative Joint Collaboration Agreement**

Appendix C **Textbook Features That College Students Do and Don't Find Helpful**

The information in this appendix was abstracted from the responses of 34 undergraduate students to a structured interview.

Appendix D **Resources for Academic Authors**

An annotated listing of books (and other publications), organizations, databases, and vendors.

COMPETING BOOKS

There are many books that focus on authoring and publishing trade books. Only a few (including *An Author's Guide to Scholarly Publishing* from Princeton University Press) focus on authoring and publishing scholarly books—intended mainly for scholars rather than students or working professionals. With the possible exception of a book that was self-published by a professor at the University of Wisconsin about 10 years ago, no book currently "in print" focuses on authoring and publishing textbooks and other educational intellectual property. A preliminary draft of this book has been purchased by about 25 college libraries and has been used as a "handout" in my authoring workshops.

SAMPLE CHAPTER

[Chapter 1 was inserted here.]

ABOUT THE AUTHOR

Franklin H. Silverman is a Professor of Speech Pathology at Marquette University (Milwaukee, Wisconsin) and a Clinical Professor of Rehabilitation Medicine at the Medical College of Wisconsin (Wauwatosa, Wisconsin). He has authored more than 150 papers in professional journals and six books: *Legal-Ethical Considerations, Restrictions, and Obligations for Clinicians Who Treat Communicative Disorders* (Second Edition, 1992); *Speech, Language, and Hearing Disorders* (Second Edition, 1995); *Communication for the Speechless* (Third Edition, 1995); *Stuttering and Other Fluency Disorders* (Second Edition, 1996); *Computer Applications for Augmenting the Management of Speech, Language, and Hearing Disorders* (Second Edition, 1997); and *Research Design and Evaluation in Speech-Language Pathology and Audiology* (Fourth Edition, 1998). One of his books has been a main selection and three have been alternate selections in professional book clubs. Translations of several of his books have been published and two are currently being translated: *Stuttering and Other Fluency Disorders* into Greek and *Communication for the Speechless* into Arabic. Dr. Silverman is a Fellow of the American Speech-Language-Hearing Association and a recipient of the Marquette University Faculty Award for Teaching Excellence. For the past ten years, he has been offering workshops for persons contemplating authoring textbooks or professional reference books under the auspices of the Text and Academic Authors Association. Dr. Silverman is a staff columnist for *The Academic Author* and the vice president/president-elect of the Text and Academic Authors Association.

APPENDIX B
A Representative Joint Collaboration Agreement[1]

AGREEMENT made as of the _____ day of _____, 19__ by and between _____ of _____ (herein called "_____") and _____ of _____ (herein called "_____"):

WHEREAS, the parties desire to collaborate on a project tentatively titled "_____" (hereinafter called the "Work") the content of which they agree will be:

NOW, THEREFORE, in consideration of the premise and of the mutual promises and undertakings herein contained, and for other good and valuable consideration, the receipt of which is hereby acknowledged, the parties agree as follows:

1. The parties agree to make themselves available to each other at times and places mutually agreeable to discuss the Work.

2. The parties agree that _____'s primary responsibilities with respect to the Work shall be:
and _____'s responsibilities with respect to the Work shall be:

3. The parties will use their best efforts to complete a manuscript satisfactory to both and ready for submission by_____.

4. The parties contemplate the completed manuscript will be approximately _____ words/pages in length [and will contain _____ illustrations if appropriate].

5. The parties agree that both of them will be involved in the negotiation of any contract(s) for publication or for any other exploitation of the Work, that both will be listed as authors on any such contract(s), and that both will execute any such contract(s).

6. The parties intend that their contributions to the Work be merged into inseparable or interdependent parts of a unitary whole, so that the work shall be a joint work under Section 101 of the Copyright Act of 1976 of which the parties shall be co-authors.

1. E. Gabriel Perle and John Taylor Williams, *The Publishing Law Handbook*, 2d ed. (Englewood Cliffs, NJ: Prentice-Hall, 1992).

7. The parties hereto shall be co-owners of the copyright in the Work and all material prepared in connection with the Work and any registration of copyright in the Work shall be in the names of both _____ and _____.

8. _____ and _____ shall receive equal credit as authors. _____'s name shall appear first and each name shall appear in type of equal size.

9. All expenses necessary to preparation of the Work and to the negotiation of contracts for exploitation of the Work shall be shared equally by the parties or in such other proportions as the parties may agree upon in a writing signed by both.

10. All income accruing from any exploitation of the Work including, but not limited to, any contract with a Publisher shall be divided equally between the parties, and all contracts relating to exploitation of the Work shall provide for equal royalty payments as well as statements from the payor to each party.

11. The parties agree each will promptly review the copyedited manuscript and proofs.

12. If at any time the parties cannot agree on editorial matters relating to the Work, the parties will attempt to negotiate such differences. If they cannot resolve such differences after thirty (30) days, either party may terminate this agreement by written notice to the other and reconciliation of any unequal expenses *or* the parties shall appoint a mutually acceptable third party to arbitrate such editorial dispute and the parties shall agree to abide promptly by the determination of the arbitrator. In the event of such termination, neither party will make use of any of the material prepared in connection with the Work in any stage without the written consent of the other. Should termination of this agreement result in cancellation of any contract pursuant to which any advance was paid, each party shall be responsible for repayment of his/her share of such advance. Should such termination of this agreement result in a breach of contract with a publisher or other licensee of the Work and suit is instituted for such breach, the parties shall share equally the cost of defense and any damages awarded.

13. The parties agree to share equally the author's responsibilities of warranty and indemnity as expressed in any contract for the exploitation of the Work, including reasonable attorney's fees, except that in any instance where any breach is the result of negligence of one of the parties (including, but not limited to, failure to obtain permissions or other unauthorized use of copyrighted material) then such party will be

solely responsible for any costs or damages incurred by the Publisher or any licensee of the Work and by the non-responsible party.

14. The parties agree neither will incorporate material based on or derived from the Work in any subsequent work without the consent of the other.

15. Any controversy or claim arising out of or relating to this agreement or any breach thereof shall be settled by arbitration in accordance with the Rules of the American Arbitration Association of the City of _____, and any award rendered by said arbitrators shall be treated as a final and non-appealable judgment of any court having jurisdiction thereof. The preceding sentence shall not apply to disputes concerning the editorial content of the Work.

16. If either party should die, become incapacitated, or for any other reason reasonably beyond his/her control be unable to complete such party's responsibilities with respect to the Work prior to the completion of the Work (the "Non-Participating Party"), the other party (the "Participating Party") may either:

a. complete the Work (both text and illustrations) himself or herself, in which case the Non-Participating Party's share of the income accruing from the exploitation of the Work shall be proportionate to the amount of the Non-Participating Party's written contribution to the completed Work (but in no event more than half), or

b. retain a third party or parties to complete the Work (both text and illustrations), in which case the reasonable compensation to such third party or parties for completing the Work shall be deducted from the Non-Participating Party's share of the income accruing from the exploitation of the Work, provided further that the Participating Party shall determine what copyright interest, if any, said third party or parties shall receive.

In either case, the Participating Party may make changes in and edit materials previously prepared; the Participating Party may alone negotiate and contract for the publication and other exploitation of the Work and generally act with regard to the Work as though the Participating Party were the sole author; and the Participating Party shall furnish the Non-Participating Party (or that Party's estate) with a copy of each contract relating to the Work so entered into by the Participating Party.

17. If, after completion of the Work, either party dies, the survivor shall have the right alone to negotiate and contract for the publication and other exploitation of the Work; make revisions in any subsequent editions and generally act with regard thereto as if he/she were the sole author, except that the remaining party shall cause the deceased party's share of the proceeds as provided hereunder to be paid to him/her or to their estate, as the case may be, and shall furnish to him/her or their estate copies of all contracts made by the surviving party pertaining to the Work.

18. This agreement, unless otherwise terminated under the terms hereof, shall continue for the life of any copyright in the Work.

19. This agreement shall enure to the benefit of, and shall be binding upon, the executors, administrators, heirs and assigns of the parties.

20. This agreement constitutes the entire understanding of the parties. It may be amended or modified only in writing signed by the parties, and shall be governed by the laws of the state of _____.

In witness whereof, the parties hereunto have set their respective hands and seals as of the day and year first above written.

By_____

_____

APPENDIX C
Permission Forms

This appendix contains representative permission forms for reproducing photographs in which people appear and copyrighted material. The former is sometimes referred to as a model release form. The model release form reproduced here was adapted from one developed by the American Society of Magazine Photographers. Both are discussed in chapter 6.

MODEL RELEASE FORM

For valuable consideration received [a copy of the photograph(s)], I hereby grant to _____ ("Author") and his/her legal representatives and assigns, the irrevocable and unrestricted right to use and publish photographs in which I am included in a book on _____; to alter the same without restriction; and to copyright the same. I hereby release Author and his/her legal representatives and assigns from all claims and liability relating to said photograph(s).

Name (Print) _____ Date _____

Signature _____ Phone _____

Address _____

City _____ State ____ ZIP_____

If Minor, Signature of Parent/Guardian _____

Witness _____

PERMISSION FORM FOR COPYRIGHTED MATERIAL

Date:

Address:

PERMISSIONS EDITOR:

I am preparing a book on "Authoring Textbooks and Other Academic and Professional Books and Materials" to be published by Praeger on or about August 1998. My book will be approximately 200 pages and will be issued in a simultaneous hardcover and paperbound edition. Trade sales will be negligible.

May I please have your permission to include the following material from:

in my book and in future revisions and editions thereof, including non-exclusive world rights in all languages. These rights will in no way restrict republication of your material in any form by you or by others authorized by you. If you do not control these rights in their entirety, please let me know to whom else I must write.

Unless you indicate otherwise, I will use the following credit line:

I would greatly appreciate your consent to this request. Please complete and return the release form below. A copy of this letter is enclosed for your files.

Sincerely,

Franklin H. Silverman, Ph.D. Dept. of Speech
Pathology, Marquette University, Milwaukee, WI 53201–1881

I (we) grant permission for the use requested above.   Date:_____
Name/Title_____
Company _____
Address_____

_____

APPENDIX D
Textbook Features That College Students Do and Don't Find Helpful

Consumers of textbooks are students. While initial textbook adoption decisions are made by instructors, the likelihood of a textbook continuing to be adopted is influenced greatly by how students react to using it. While their attitudes toward a textbook will be influenced by its content, they will also be influenced by its appearance and organization and how it is written. Some features of a textbook's appearance, organization, and the style in which it is written are likely to cause students to react positively to it because they are *helpful to them*; others tend to have the opposite effect on their reactions to a textbook; and still others (which can add significantly to the cost of a textbook) tend to have little, or no, effect on their reactions to one. It obviously is important, therefore, that authors of textbooks be aware of features that do and those that do not tend to be helpful to students.

To begin to categorize these features, 34 students at Marquette University were interviewed about their reactions to a number of them. The interviewing was done by my research assistant, Gabriele Merz-Johnson, who at the time was a masters-level graduate student. Most of the students were undergraduates who were enrolled in an introductory public-speaking course. There were students in this group who were majoring in the sciences, the humanities, and professional training programs (e.g., engineering and business administration). The students were asked to respond to a number of open-ended questions, and their responses to them were recorded on audio tape. Some excerpts from their responses that I thought could be helpful to authors are reproduced here. The order in which they are presented is not intended to communicate how important I regard them as being.

While the focus of this survey was textbooks, many of the respondents' comments can contribute to making other types of educational and professional books and materials more helpful as well. Hopefully, at least a few of these comments will resonate for you in a manner that will enable you to make your book or material at least a little more helpful than it would have been otherwise.

Of the textbooks you used while in college, think of the ones that were MOST helpful to you. What characteristics do they share?

- They are very well organized. It is clear what each chapter talks about. There are a lot of headings and subheadings and maybe even comments on the side [in a narrow column on the left side of the page] that summarize or indicate what is being talked about.

- I find it helpful if there is space, at least 1.5 inches, on the sides of pages in which I can write. As I read, I like to make little summaries for myself of the main points.

- I like summaries at the ends of chapters in which the main points are listed.

- I find it interesting, too, if there are references for further reading. I feel that in textbooks things are just touched on. Authors take information from other sources—for example, research articles. Sometimes I would like to be able to take a look at them myself.

- I like illustrations if they are supportive to the text I am reading and are [on a page] close to what I am reading so that as I'm reading, I can easily refer back and forth.

- I find photographs and drawings useful when something is being explained about a complex instrument with which I am not familiar. It can tell me what the different buttons are for.

- I find figures and charts, such as flowcharts, useful that summarize things that are talked about in the text.

- Textbooks are most helpful to me when they begin each chapter with an outline of what is going to be covered in it and end each chapter with a summary of what was covered in it in essay form.

- I like it when the definitions are highlighted—boldfaced or italicized. [Note: Almost all of the students made a similar comment.]

- Pictures definitely help. They make the material seem less imposing. If I'm reading page after page of writing, when I come to a picture it's really nice because it's a page or part of a page that I don't have to read. Somehow, they make the task of reading a textbook seem less overwhelming.

- I particularly like textbooks in which authors relate personal experiences or tell stories about how the information they are presenting applies to everyday life.

- Using examples that are humorous to students can help to make a text for what most would consider a boring course—for example, a theology one—interesting.

- I am usually able to understand graphs better when they are in color. I also tend to regard books as being more up-to-date when the graphs are in color.

Of the textbooks you used while in college, think of the ones that were LEAST helpful to you. What characteristics do they share?

- I find it cumbersome when references are given in numbered footnotes and the footnotes are in the back of the book. However, I do not find it cumbersome if they are at the bottom of the page on which the studies are cited.

- I find it difficult to concentrate for page after page without having the material subdivided in some way—for example, by headings and subheadings. [Note: Almost all of the students made a similar comment.]

- Sometimes I have the feeling that photographs and drawings—including cartoons—are just being included to make a book look nicer. I have this feeling when they really don't seem to support anything that is being discussed in the text.

- I don't find photographs helpful that show an instrument being used in which it is difficult to see the instrument. This is particularly annoying if I can't see the instrument well enough to understand the description of it given in the text.

- I get turned off by photographs that are not recent, judging by the way people are dressed or something else. Their presence suggests to me that the book is not up-to-date.

- If there are a lot of references to papers more than five years old, I get the feeling that the book is not current. In my field, things are changing rapidly.

- I usually don't pay attention to illustrations and graphs. I just skim right over them.

- I find it tedious when authors cite one research study or case study after another.

- It tends to be disruptive if the author indicates that something mentioned will be described in a later chapter. I often don't know whether to try to find it or to keep on reading.

- I find that textbooks which are printed in small type with narrow margins do not hold my attention well, particularly if they are in technical subjects.

Have you ever had a textbook that was printed in more than one color? If "yes," did this feature really make it a more useful learning tool? Why?

- I think it can help, but it can be distracting if many colors are used.
- I like it when color type is used for highlighting—for example, for highlighting definitions.
- I have had textbooks in which color was used effectively as background for setting off material that is relevant to the text, but not a part of it—for example, case studies.
- It definitely helps to hold my attention longer. It makes textbooks less boring. My theology books, for example, don't have any color at all—just writing. I think that they would hold my attention longer if they were made more attractive—for example, through the use of color.
- Color may be clearer than type size for indicating various levels of headings—for example, main headings could be red, first-level subheadings blue, and second-level ones green. In order to reliably interpret type size, it is necessary to search for headings to compare with. It, also, may be clearer than type size for indicating key terms and their definitions.

Have you ever had a textbook that had color photographs and/or illustrations (rather than black-and-white ones)? If "yes," did this feature really make it a more useful learning tool? Why?

- It made a book with anatomical diagrams more useful because the presence of color allowed information to be communicated more clearly than would have been the case otherwise since there were a number of structures depicted in them.
- Color photographs look nicer than black-and-white ones, but they usually don't communicate any more information.
- Color photographs make books more reader friendly. They are more appealing to the eye than black-and-white ones.
- It doesn't make that much difference, though color photographs tend to hold my attention for a little longer than black-and-white ones.

- Our generation tends to view color photographs as the norm and black-and-white ones as old fashioned—not up-to-date. We, therefore, respond more positively to [pay more attention to] color photographs even though black-and-white ones convey [just] as well what the author is trying to communicate. [Note: Many of the students made similar comments.]

What characteristics of a textbook author's writing style tend to "turn you on" and "turn you off"?

- I feel that the language used should be simpler than in a research article. Terms should be explained as you go along.

- I like a writing style in which sentences are short and concise.

- I find it helpful when the author has transition paragraphs between topics in which he or she indicates what will be discussed next.

- I sometimes find it distracting if the author frequently has long lists of references—authors and years—in parenthesis at the ends of sentences. Also, I don't like it when authors have references in footnotes and the footnotes are at the end of the book. It's okay, however, if the footnotes are at the bottoms of pages on which articles and books are cited.

- I like it when authors repeat main points. I have a very short attention span when reading textbooks so the repetition helps me out a lot.

- It makes it less boring for me when there are a lot of examples, particularly ones that relate to things I'm interested in.

- I find textbooks most helpful when they are written on a level that I can understand and when they are written in a way that makes them seem relevant to things I am interested in in the real world.

- I don't like textbooks that contain a lot of fluffy stuff. By this I mean such things as big words that aren't defined and lots of clauses and run-on sentences. I prefer sentences to be short, simple, and to the point.

- I like it when important terms are in bold print rather than italicized. Bold print is easier to spot.

- I would much rather read a textbook that was written in the first person. It seems more like someone is talking right to me and more like they have an actual interest in the subject rather than just throwing down a bunch of statistical facts to spew out to a bunch of students who don't really want to learn them.

- I like it when paragraphs are relatively short and make a single point.

- I've had several textbooks in which there were definitions of technical terms in the margins [in a narrow column on the left side of the page]. This was quite helpful.

- I find it easier to understand points [e.g., the five characteristics of something] when they are presented in list form rather than in paragraph form.

- I like it when authors tell you what they are going to tell you, then tell you, and then tell you what they told you. The repetition helps to pound the points into your brain.

- If a matter is controversial, I find it helpful when the author presents the various points of view and then indicates which one he or she feels makes the most sense and why. It upsets me if the author gives no opinion since I know that he or she must have one.

What organizational features of textbooks (e.g., headings and subheadings) tend to "turn you on" and "turn you off"?

- I like comments in the margin that summarize important points. It helps me to know what to focus on as I am reading.

- Organization and coherency are of number one importance. If it is coherent, I can read it without having to search for what they are trying to tell me or search for definitions.

- What turns me off is when you're given bunches of information that is really in no structured form—for example, when the author goes from one topic to the next without any real transition.

- I like a lot of subsections. It doesn't seem as overwhelming if the sections are relatively short.

- I like the information to be broken down into small units—subsections—because it indicates to me where it is safe to take a break in my reading.

- I like it when material within chapters is printed in close to outline form—the way it is in some computer software manuals. It makes it clearer what the main points are and how they relate to each other.

- I'd rather have a lot of short chapters than a few relatively long ones. I like to read a whole chapter at a time. If the chapters seem to be long, I'm likely to put off reading them. Also, if they are relatively long, it makes it more difficult to maintain concentration.

- I find it helpful if there is a detailed table of contents—one that includes main chapter headings and subheadings.

- Color-coding can be an effective way to signal the beginnings of sections, subsections, and other features. The coding can be communicated by the color of the type, the color of the background, or the color of the paper on which material is printed. For example, the glossary can be printed on a different color paper to make it easier to find.

- It turns me off if there are too many levels of subsections—more than three. It makes it hard to synthesize the material and figure out what the big picture is supposed to be.

How helpful have chapter summaries been to you? Why?

- I find chapter summaries useful for studying for tests. If they do a good job covering the main points, I can tell by reading them how well I understand the material. [Note: Almost all of the students made a comment similar to this.]

- I usually read the summary before I read the chapter. After I read the chapter, I read the summary again. It's helpful when you're going through a chapter if you know what the main points are going to be. Chapter summaries give me a guide to go by.

- I like it when the chapter is outlined at the beginning and summarized at the end. It gives you an overview and a conclusion.

- I find chapter summaries especially helpful for reviewing if the order of topics in the summary corresponds to that in the chapter. If you don't remember certain points, it is easier to locate them if this was done.

- Chapter summaries aren't too helpful in math textbooks. Problems in which you have to apply what was discussed are better for this purpose.

How helpful have glossaries and indexes been to you? What could be done to make them more helpful?

- I find it cumbersome to have to go to the back of the book to look up terms. I prefer to have the term defined on the page on which it occurs.

- I find glossaries useful. I use them more like a dictionary and for reviewing for tests. By scanning the terms, I often can tell how well I understand the material. [Note: Almost all of the students made a similar comment.]
- One reason why indexes are useful is because all too often professors cover material in their lectures that is in the book, but not in the chapters they are lecturing on.
- Often there is more than one index—an index for authors and an index for topics. In my business books there is often also an index for companies. And sometimes you just flip to the wrong index. It just makes me crazy. Sometimes I wonder why they just can't combine them.
- I prefer to have a glossary all in one place at the end of the book rather than one for each chapter. It makes it easier if you remember reading a definition, but not in which chapter you found it.
- Some indexes when they list pages for a term will indicate the one [as a subheading] on which it is defined. I find this very helpful.
- I don't like it when there is no glossary. I rely on them for defining unfamiliar terms.
- I use the index as a glossary. By looking a term up as it is used in various contexts I often can get a better understanding of its meaning than I could from a typical glossary definition.
- One textbook glossary that I thought was really good after each definition listed pages on which the term was referred to.
- Glossaries should either be thorough or not there at all. If I find a few times that terms that I feel should be there aren't there, I usually stop using it.
- If terms are highlighted [boldfaced or italicized] in the book, they should be included in the glossary.

Have any of the textbooks you've used been written at too high or too low a level? If "yes," what makes you judge them in this way?

- Many are written at too high a level but few at too low a one. I appreciate having a textbook that is easy to read—one in which I understand the words used. [Note: Almost all of the students made statements like this.]
- I don't like it so much if the author seems to be saying exactly the same thing three or four times. I'm reading—not in a lecture. If I don't understand what I read the first time, I can reread it.

- Some of my textbooks have been written at too high a level. They assume that you have information from previous courses that you don't have. I have frequently found this to be the case in math textbooks.

- More of the textbooks I've used—particularly those for courses not in my major—have been written at too high than at too low a level. They assumed that I had information that I didn't and they contained a lot of words—terms—with which I was not familiar and which were not adequately defined in the text.

- I have never objected to a textbook that was written at a low level—one that was easy to read.

- I would much rather read a book that was written at too low a level than one that was written at too high a one. Though the writer may think that I'm a real idiot because he [or she] has to explain the same thing five times, I'd much rather get frustrated that way than read something at so high a level that I really feel like an idiot.

Have any of the textbooks you've used had sidebars? If "yes," did this feature make them a more useful learning tool? Why?

- I find sidebars interesting, but also a little distracting. I either read over them and then go back and look at them or I don't even look at them. I particularly react negatively to sidebars when the author says nothing in the text about what I am supposed to get out of them.

- The locations of sidebars influence my reaction to them. I am more likely to react negatively [to] the sidebars if their location is such that their presence disrupts the flow of my reading of the text. If relatively long ones were at the ends of chapters, I would be less likely to find them objectionable.

- A few of my texts have had definitions as sidebars. This feature was helpful.

- I really find sidebars interesting if they contain case studies or examples of material being talked about in the text being applied in real life.

- Textbooks in the dryer subjects—ones in which I am not really interested—should make more use of sidebars, particularly ones that relate the material to my world. This would tend to increase my interest in the subject and, consequently, the amount of time I would spend with the book.

- I read [in my educational psychology book] all the way down to the bottom of the page and the sentence wasn't complete. On the top of the next page was a sidebar containing examples. While deciding whether to read it or not, I forgot the point the author was making. If there are going to be sidebars in a chapter, they should be placed where they won't distract students.

- Some sidebars pose questions that make you think about the information you are reading. I find these helpful because they challenge you to apply it to other situations.

- In one of my textbooks full-page sidebars were printed on a different color paper. This was effective for differentiating sidebars from text.

- I like sidebars because they provide a break. The material in them is usually more interesting and easier to understand than that in the text.

What other suggestions do you have for improving the quality of textbooks?

- It is helpful in photographs if the part that you are supposed to focus on [the part that is important] stands out. I've seen this done by graying-over [airbrushing] the unimportant parts.

- I like it when there is information given about the author. It gives you an image that you can keep in mind while you are reading. It tends to make the interaction between you and the author more personal.

- I like it when books are printed on paper that can be written on with a pencil. Those printed on a glossy paper are usually difficult to write on with one.

- One thing that really bothers me are oversize textbooks—ones that are 8-by-10 inches or larger. They are more awkward to carry around than normal size ones. I tend to avoid taking a book home to study from if it looks like it would be awkward to carry. Also, seeing a large page in front of you makes the material seem more overwhelming.

- I particularly have difficulty maintaining attention when I'm reading textbooks for courses that are not in my major, such as those in philosophy and theology. It is probably more important that books for non-majors be written in an interesting manner than those for majors. One way this can be done is to include lots of examples that would be relevant to students regardless of their major.

- Illustrations help psychologically to motivate me to not put off doing reading assignments. If I see that a number of the pages that have been assigned contain photographs or drawings, it makes the assignment seem easier—more doable.

- If a study is important enough to be mentioned in a textbook, it should be summarized, not just cited.

- Even though I usually overlook graphs, they are helpful to me in a way. They help me remember where information is located. For example, I recall that something was discussed on the page opposite a particular figure.

- I like it best when tables and figures are either on the page on which they are referred to or on that opposite it. I find it disruptive when I can't see the figure or table and text referring to it at the same time.

- Personal examples help. I like it when the personality and experiences of the author come through. I also find lectures more interesting when these come through.

- Just staring at words, page after page after page, turns me off. It has to be broken up in some way—for example, by illustrations—to hold my interest.

- Make few assumptions about previous knowledge. Authors often assume that students enrolling in a course have knowledge that they don't. They may have had it at one time, but didn't retain it. Some review is essential!

- It is important to write a textbook for non-majors differently than one for majors. One reason is that non-majors may only be taking the course for which it is intended because they are required to do so. They may not be interested in the subject. They may even assume that they will not be able to understand the material. This is particularly likely to be the case if the course is a math or science one. It is important that such books be written in a way that can be easily understood by persons who have no previous knowledge of the subject. It is also important that they be written in a way that is likely to generate enthusiasm for the subject.

- It might be helpful at the beginnings or ends of chapters to include a list of technical terms that are dealt with in it. These could help students decide when preparing for an exam whether they need to reread a chapter.

- Students may spend more time reading paperback books than hardcover ones. Part of the reason is that they may consider hardcover ones to be more awkward to take with them than paperback ones because they are larger and weigh more. The more often they take a book with them, the more time they are likely to spend reading it.

- It is important that all pictures have captions and that the captions clearly explain what the student is supposed to attend to in them.

- Study questions that don't just ask for facts that are in the chapter are helpful because they make you think about implications of the information and to integrate it. They also motivate you to acquire more information. If I can't adequately answer a question, I usually try to find the information needed to answer it, regardless of whether the professor requires me to do so.

- Authors sometimes seem to forget that textbooks are supposed to be learning tools rather than literary works. While presenting material in semi-outline form is not appropriate for a literary work, it may be for a textbook. By semi-outline form, I mean the style used in most computer software manuals.

- If there are calculation exercises, answers should be given in the book. If they are only given in the instructor's manual, this reduces their value to students who want to check themselves on how well they understand how to do the calculations.

- I like textbooks best in which you feel that the author is trying to communicate to you rather than just rattle off facts.

- Package foreign language textbooks with tapes that illustrate pronunciation.

- Color makes a textbook seem of higher quality. It makes you feel that your money has been better spent.

APPENDIX E
Standard Proof Correction Notation

Symbol	Meaning	Symbol	Meaning
∧	Correct as margin indicates	≡	Under word means caps
stet	Let it stand	═	Under word small caps
✗	Battered letter	—	Under word means Italic
≣	Straighten lines	rom	Change to Roman
⫽⫽	Unevenly spaced-line up	ital	Change to Italic
No ¶	No paragraph	bf	Bold face
out see copy	Omission here	⌄	Comma
¶	Paragraph	;/	Semicolon
tr	Transpose	:	Colon
ℓ	Delete as indicated	⊙	Period
ℓ	Delete—close up	?/	Interrogation mark
⑤	Upside down	!/	Exclamation mark
◡	Close up	/=	Hyphen
#	Insert space	'	Apostrophe
⊥	Push down this space	⁵/⁵	Quotation marks
▫	Indent one em	⌄	Superior letter or figure
⊐⊏	Move to left/or right	⌃	Inferior letter or figure
⌐/⌐	Raise/or lower	⊏⊐	Brackets
⫽⫽⫽	Hair space letters	(/)	Parenthesis
wf	Wrong font	1/m	One-em dash
Sc	Small capitals	2/m	Two-em dash
Caps	Capitals	lc	Lower case
C + Sc	Caps—small caps	OK?	Is this right?

APPENDIX F
Common Characteristics of Best-Selling Textbooks[1]

1. They dominate their field through two or more editions.
   a. They are perceived as pedagogically sound.
   b. They are prestigious, irrespective of the level of sophistication.
   c. They enhance and complement the instructor's lectures.
   d. They are nonthreatening to instructors and students alike.
2. They are written with precision, accuracy, and, if they involve analysis, that degree of rigor appropriate to the audience.
3. They are written with verve, and thus conducive to a reading.
   a. They reward the reader in that he or she intuitively senses the reward of learning.
   b. The inferential leaps from concept to concept are sufficiently challenging so as not to bore the better students, or to intimidate the average students.
   c. The interstitial material is such that the reader can make a smooth transition from paragraph to paragraph, chapter to chapter, and so forth.
4. Their table of contents, index, and, if appropriate, glossary are exhaustive and precise.
5. They incorporate research findings, heretofore restricted to journals or research papers, if those ideas are now established theory. If the findings are speculative, they are so designated with a reason given for their presentation in the book.
6. They use color to enhance learning.
   a. Gratuitous use of color increases cost of publication.
   b. Judicious use of color clarifies learning, as when it is employed in shading three-dimensional illustrations, setting off principles, and so forth.

---

1. Adapted from a presentation by Peter D. Quass of the Academic Authors Agency (P.O. Box 3699, Manhattan Beach, CA 90266-1699) at the 1997 annual convention of the Text and Academic Authors Association.

7. Their problem sets are progressively more difficult and are located at the end of chapters and/or sections, are cumulative in some instances to provide a summary to date, and may very well glimpse ahead to new material.

8. Their cases can involve a single concept and be concise. The cases can be comprehensive but rarely complex. A single case study can run throughout the text.

9. They are recognized as a reference source and foundation for subsequent courses and careers.

10. They have a rising sales curve through each edition.

11. They are eagerly sought by used-book wholesalers, at a premium price.

12. They are few in number.

References and Resources

Applebaum, J. (1988). *How to Get Happily Published* (3rd ed.). New York: Harper & Row.

Applebaum, J., & Evans, N. (1978). *How to Get Happily Published.* New York: Harper & Row.

Balkin, R. (1981). *A Writer's Guide to Book Publishing.* New York: Hawthorn.

———. (1985). *How to Understand and Negotiate a Book Contract or Magazine Agreement.* Cincinnati, OH: Writer's Digest Books.

Beale, S., & Cavuoto, J. (1989). *The Scanner Book.* Torrance, CA: Micro Publishing Press.

Bell, H. W. (1985). *How to Get Your Book Published: An Insider's View.* Cincinnati, OH: Writer's Digest Books.

Bennett, H. Z., & Larsen, M. (1988). *How to Write with a Collaborator.* Cincinnati, OH: Writer's Digest Books.

Blue, M. (1990). *By the Book: Legal ABCs for the Printed Word.* Flagstaff, AZ: Northland.

Brechner, I. (1992, April). Twelve compelling reasons for authors and publishers to create software enhancements to books. *TAA Report,* 6(2), 8–9.

Brownstone, D. M., & Frank, I. M. (1985). *The Self-Publishing Handbook.* New American Library.

Bunnin, B., & Beren, P. (1988). *The Writer's Legal Companion*. Reading, MA: Addison-Wesley.

Burgett, G. (1989). *Self-Publishing to Tightly Targeted Markets*. Santa Monica, CA: Communication Unlimited, P.O. Box 6405.

Crawford, T. (1977). *The Writer's Legal Guide*. New York, NY: Hawthorn Books.

Delbert, W. (1991, July). Who really writes elementary school textbooks? *TAA Report*, 5(3), 19–20.

Derricourt, R. (1996). *An Author's Guide to Scholarly Publishing*. Princeton, NJ: Princeton University Press.

Diamond, N. (1983). *Publishing at Prentice-Hall: From Manuscript to Bound Book*. Englewood Cliffs, NJ: Prentice-Hall.

Dible, D. M. (1978). *What Everybody Should Know About Patents, Trademarks, and Copyrights*. Fairfield, CA: Entrepreneur Press.

Fields' Reference Book for Non-sexist Words and Phrases. (1987). Raleigh, NC: Fields' Enterprises, 3056 Granville Drive.

Henderson, B. (Ed.) (1980). *The Publish-It-Yourself Handbook: Literary Tradition and How-To*. Wainscott, NY: Pushcart Press.

Herman, J., & Adams, D. M. (1993). *Write the Perfect Book Proposal*. New York: John Wiley.

Holt, R. L. (1985). *How to Publish, Promote, and Sell Your Own Book*. New York: St. Martin's Press.

Keedy, M. (1989, April). Let's get royalty rates back where they belong. *TAA Report*, 3(2), 2.

———. (1992, January). Where have all the authors gone? *TAA Report*, 6(1), 2, 6.

Kelper, M. L. (1990). *An Illustrated Handbook of Desktop Publishing and Typesetting* (2d ed.). Summit, PA: Tab Books.

King, L. S. (1991). *Why Not Say It Clearly? A Guide to Expository Writing*. Boston: Little, Brown.

Kozak, E. M. (1990a). *Every Writer's Guide to Copyright and Publishing Law*. New York: Henry Holt.

———. (1990b). *From Pen to Print: The Secrets of Getting Published*. New York: Henry Holt.

Krementz, J. (1996). *The Writer's Desk*. New York: Random House.

Kremer, J. (1990). *1001 Ways to Market Your Book*. Fairfield, IA: Ad-Lib Publications.

Larsen, M. (1985). *How to Write a Book Proposal*. Cincinnati, OH: Writer's Digest Books.

Levine, M. L. (1988). *Negotiating a Book Contract*. New York: Moyer Bell Limited.

Linden, D. W. (1992, March 16). Cooking the books. *Forbes*, pp. 130–131.

Luey, B. (1987). *Handbook for Academic Authors*. New York: Cambridge University Press.

MacDonald, W. D. (1983). *Author's Guide to College Textbook Publishing* [Pamphlet]. New York: Association of American Publishers.

McGraw-Hill Book Company. (n.d.). *Guidelines for Bias-Free Publishing*. Hightstown, NJ: McGraw-Hill.

Meyer, C. (1984). *The Writer's Survival Manual*. New York: Bantam Books.

Michener, J. (1992). *James A. Michener's Writer's Handbook*. New York: Random House.

Miles, J. (1987). *Design for Desktop Publishing*. San Francisco: Chronicle Books.

Miller, C., & Swift, K. (1988). *The Handbook of Nonsexist Writing*. New York: Harper & Row.

Mozley, Joseph M. (1992). *Publish, Don't Perish: The Scholar's Guide to Academic Writing and Publishing*. Westport, CT: Praeger Publishers.

Mueller, L. W. (1978). *How to Publish Your Own Book*. Detroit: Harlo Press.

Novick, K. P., & Chasen, J. S. (1984). *The Rights of Authors and Artists*. New York: Bantam Books.

Powell, W. W. (1985). *Getting into Print: The Decision-Making Process in Scholarly Publishing*. Chicago: University of Chicago Press.

Poynter, D. (1989). *The Self-Publishing Manual*. Santa Barbara, CA: Para Publishing.

Pressing Business: An Organizational Manual for Independent Publishers. (1984). New York: Volunteer Lawyers for the Arts, 1285 Avenue of the Americas.

Principles of Good Writing. (1969). Westport, CT: Famous Writers School.

Rodberg, L. R. (1992). Getting your copy-editing budget's worth. *TAA Report*, 6(2), 13.

Schultz, D. (1990). *Tools of the Writer's Trade*. New York: HarperCollins.

Silverman, F. H. (1992). *Legal-Ethical Considerations, Restrictions, and Obligations for Clinicians Who Treat Communicative Disorders*. Springfield, IL: Charles Thomas.

———. (1996). Personal involvement in the development of programs for persons with disabilities. In Roy I. Brown, David Baine, & Aldred Neufeldt (Eds.), *Beyond Basic Care: Special Education and Community Rehabilitation in Low Income Countries*. North York, Ontario: Captus Press, 254–260.

Strong, W. S. (1984). *The Copyright Book: A Practical Guide* (2d ed.). Cambridge, MA: MIT Press.

Strunk, W., Jr., & White, E. B. (1979). *The Elements of Style* (3d ed.). New York: Macmillan.

Van Til, W. (1986). *Writing for Professional Publication* (2d ed.). Boston: Allyn & Bacon.

Zinsser, W. (1988). *Writing to Learn*. New York: Harper & Row.

Index

About the Author

FRANKLIN H. SILVERMAN is Professor of Speech Pathology at Marquette University and Clinical Professor of Rehabilitation Medicine at the Medical College of Wisconsin. He has authored more than a dozen text/professional books and more than 125 articles in professional journals. He is currently President of the Text and Academic Authors Association.

ISBN 0-275-96159-1

90000>

9 780275 961596

HARDCOVER BAR CODE